THE IRAN–NORTH KOREA STRATEGIC ALLIANCE

JOINT HEARING

BEFORE THE

SUBCOMMITTEE ON TERRORISM, NONPROLIFERATION, AND TRADE

SUBCOMMITTEE ON ASIA AND THE PACIFIC

AND THE

SUBCOMMITTEE ON THE MIDDLE EAST AND NORTH AFRICA

OF THE

COMMITTEE ON FOREIGN AFFAIRS HOUSE OF REPRESENTATIVES

ONE HUNDRED FOURTEENTH CONGRESS

FIRST SESSION

———

JULY 28, 2015

———

Serial No. 114–76

———

Printed for the use of the Committee on Foreign Affairs

Available via the World Wide Web: http://www.foreignaffairs.house.gov/ or http://www.gpo.gov/fdsys/

———

U.S. GOVERNMENT PUBLISHING OFFICE

95–694PDF   WASHINGTON : 2015

For sale by the Superintendent of Documents, U.S. Government Publishing Office
Internet: bookstore.gpo.gov   Phone: toll free (866) 512–1800; DC area (202) 512–1800
Fax: (202) 512–2104   Mail: Stop IDCC, Washington, DC 20402–0001

COMMITTEE ON FOREIGN AFFAIRS

EDWARD R. ROYCE, California, *Chairman*

CHRISTOPHER H. SMITH, New Jersey
ILEANA ROS-LEHTINEN, Florida
DANA ROHRABACHER, California
STEVE CHABOT, Ohio
JOE WILSON, South Carolina
MICHAEL T. McCAUL, Texas
TED POE, Texas
MATT SALMON, Arizona
DARRELL E. ISSA, California
TOM MARINO, Pennsylvania
JEFF DUNCAN, South Carolina
MO BROOKS, Alabama
PAUL COOK, California
RANDY K. WEBER SR., Texas
SCOTT PERRY, Pennsylvania
RON DeSANTIS, Florida
MARK MEADOWS, North Carolina
TED S. YOHO, Florida
CURT CLAWSON, Florida
SCOTT DesJARLAIS, Tennessee
REID J. RIBBLE, Wisconsin
DAVID A. TROTT, Michigan
LEE M. ZELDIN, New York
DANIEL DONOVAN, New York

ELIOT L. ENGEL, New York
BRAD SHERMAN, California
GREGORY W. MEEKS, New York
ALBIO SIRES, New Jersey
GERALD E. CONNOLLY, Virginia
THEODORE E. DEUTCH, Florida
BRIAN HIGGINS, New York
KAREN BASS, California
WILLIAM KEATING, Massachusetts
DAVID CICILLINE, Rhode Island
ALAN GRAYSON, Florida
AMI BERA, California
ALAN S. LOWENTHAL, California
GRACE MENG, New York
LOIS FRANKEL, Florida
TULSI GABBARD, Hawaii
JOAQUIN CASTRO, Texas
ROBIN L. KELLY, Illinois
BRENDAN F. BOYLE, Pennsylvania

AMY PORTER, *Chief of Staff* THOMAS SHEEHY, *Staff Director*
JASON STEINBAUM, *Democratic Staff Director*

CONTENTS

THE IRAN–NORTH KOREA STRATEGIC ALLIANCE

TUESDAY, JULY 28, 2015

House of Representatives,
Subcommittee on Terrorism, Nonproliferation, and Trade,
Subcommittee on Asia and the Pacific and
Subcommittee on the Middle East and North Africa,
Committee on Foreign Affairs,
Washington, DC.

The subcommittees met, pursuant to notice, at 3:03 p.m., in room 2172, Rayburn House Office Building, Hon. Ted Poe [chairman of the Subcommittee on Terrorism, Nonproliferation, and Trade] presiding.

Mr. POE. The subcommittees will come to order.

Without objection, all members may have 5 days to submit statements, questions, extraneous materials for the record, subject to the length limitation in the rules.

I do want to thank especially our witnesses for being here and the members as well. This apparently is Iran day at Capitol Hill, and so we will continue the discussion of Iran.

The long history of secret cooperation between Iran and North Korea in violation of international law stretches back for decades. North Korea first sold Iran ballistic missiles during the 1980s during Iran's war with Iraq. By the end of the 1980s, North Korea and China were supplying Iran with about 70 percent of its arms. Move to the 1990s, and Iran and North Korea had moved onto working together to develop long-range ballistic missiles. North Korean long-range ballistic missiles became the basis for the Iranian Shahab missile series, which currently threatens Israel, our other Middle East allies, and even Central Europe. In fact, the intelligence community has said that missile cooperation between Iran and North Korea has provided Iran with an increase in its military capabilities. By the beginning of the 2000s, the Iranians were giving North Korea sensitive data from their own missile tests to improve the North Korean missile systems. In fact, Iranian officials have been present at nearly every major North Korean missile test.

This history of very close cooperation on ballistic missiles only has the potential to grow and deepen as a result of the Iranian nuclear deal. In 8 years, Iran will be able to freely work on its ballistic missile system. Iran was able to achieve so much in secret, thanks to its North Korean allies. We can only imagine what it will be able to do after the ban on the ballistic missile program is lifted.

There is a growing evidence that Iran and North Korea have not only been cooperating on missile programs but also in the nuclear field. The media reports, as far as back as 1993, that there are indications that the Iranians financed North Korea's nuclear program with $500 million in return for nuclear technology. South Korean news outlets rang the alarm in 2011 alleging that hundreds of North Korean nuclear and missile experts were working in Iran. One of those places that had North Korean experts working in it was Natanz, a nuclear facility where centrifuges will continue to enrich uranium under the nuclear deal.

Iranian defectors have also revealed a long history of North Korean experts working on the Iranian nuclear program. Just like with the missile program, Iranian officials have attended nearly every North Korean nuclear test, gleaning important information to improve their nuclear program. Last month, an Iranian opposition group claimed that nuclear expert delegations from North Korea had traveled to Iran three times this year alone. The delegations allegedly met with Iranian officials responsible for nuclear warhead design. These recent visits occurred as Iran was buckling under a serious sanctions regime.

Now that sanctions probably will be lifted and Iran will receive anywhere from $50 billion to $150 billion in what I term a signing bonus and hundreds of billions of dollars more in oil revenue, that means a lot more money to pay cash-hungry North Korea for game-changing nuclear technology and expertise.

The strong relationship between Iran and North Korea was forged in secrecy. We do not even know the full extent of their working together. What we do know is that now that the world has given the Iranian nuclear program an apparent stamp of approval, North Korea has a lot to gain from the Iranians as well.

Continued work on the Iranian nuclear program will mean more transfer of sensitive nuclear information back and forth between the two most dangerous rogue regimes in the world. A better understanding of the strategic alliance between Iran and North Korea highlights the inherent dangers of an Iranian nuclear program. Unfortunately, it appears that these dangers will only multiply as soon as the nuclear deal goes in effect.

I will now turn to the ranking member of the subcommittee, Mr. Keating from Massachusetts, for his opening statement.

Mr. KEATING. Thank you, Chairman Poe, Chairman Salmon, and Chairman Ros-Lehtinen, for conducting this joint hearing today. I would also like to thank our witnesses for being here today to discuss the relationship between Iran and North Korea.

As this morning's full committee hearing with Secretaries Kerry, Moniz, and Lew demonstrated, there are many questions that remain among members of this committee regarding the scope of the threat of Iran and North Korea. I believe that you will be able to provide valuable insight on this issue and I look forward to your testimony.

Both Iran and North Korea present national security threats to the United States and our allies. They each have a history nuclear proliferation, engage in serious human rights abuses, and are a source of instability in their respective regions. Iran is a sponsor of terrorism through illicit activities led by the Islamic Revolutionary Guard Corps and Quds Force. Most threatening is its network of partners beyond its borders and the influence that its funding and support holds over the region.

Likewise, North Korea is known to be heavily involved in transnational organized crime. Make no mistake, Iran and North Korea are dangerous actors on the world stage.

Generally, the extent to which an adversary is considered a threat can be measured by considering its capability times its intent. As we review and analyze the Joint Comprehensive Plan of Action transmitted to Congress, we must consider how a nuclear agreement with Iran would impact its capabilities and intentions beyond its borders. With this in mind, it is worth exploring whether, as some have suggested, a nuclear deal with Iran might enable and promote it to obtain nuclear or missile technology from cash-strapped North Korea.

But in doing so, we have to rely on credible evidence. For example, we know that North Korea sold Scud missiles to Iran beginning in the 1980s, and according to the U.S. intelligence community, the two countries have cooperated significantly on ballistic missile technology, but according to the Congressional Research Service, according to unclassified and declassified U.S. intelligence community assessments, and in reports of that nature, they indicate to date that there is no evidence that Iran and North Korea have engaged in nuclear-related trade or cooperation with each other.

I look forward to hearing more from our witnesses about any cooperation between Iran and North Korea with respect to nuclear or missile technology and how the Joint Comprehensive Plan of Action might affect the relationship between these two countries.

With that, I yield back.

Mr. POE. Thank the gentleman from Massachusetts.

This is a joint subcommittee hearing with three subcommittees, and all three chairs are here. I will now recognize the chairman of the Asia and the Pacific Subcommittee, Mr. Matt Salmon from Arizona, for his opening statement.

Mr. SALMON. I think there was a line in a movie like, Mr. Chairman, Madam Chairman.

Ms. ROS-LEHTINEN. Doctor, Doctor.

Mr. SALMON. Yes, Doctor, Doctor.

Anyway, it is great to be here with both of you today and to have this hearing. I would like to also thank our distinguished witnesses for coming to speak on this Iran-North Korea relationship.

As we consider the administration's Joint Comprehensive Action Plan with Iran, we have to ask, will Iran follow through with its international obligations? After hearing the administration explain the terms of the deal this morning, I can't be so sure. The deal could put Iran on a path toward developing a nuclear bomb within 10 short years. As chairman of the Asia and the Pacific Subcommittee, I am concerned with the decades-long nuclear and military cooperation between Iran and North Korea and exactly what implications the deal has on their prospects for developing nuclear weapons.

North Korea's nuclear weapons program has been the primary focus of the U.S.-North Korea policy for decades. It has tested three nuclear devices within the last 10 years and, in May 2012, declared itself a nuclear arms state. North Korea appears to be expanding its capacity to produce both plutonium and highly enriched uranium for nuclear weapons. North Korea has repeatedly emphasized the role of its nuclear weapons as a deterrent and as a means to obtain concessions and cash in exchange for technology and components.

North Korea has a track record similar to Iran of failing to meet international obligations. The February 29 of 2012 agreement committed North Korea to a moratorium on nuclear tests, long-range missile launches, and uranium enrichment at the Yongbyon facility, as well as readmission of IAEA inspectors. In return, the administration pledged 240,000 tons of food aid. The deal quickly fell apart when North Korea announced its intention to launch a long-range rocket in March, successfully doing so in December 2012.

North Korea's sales of missile technology and sharing of expertise to Iran is a major concern. Iran has cultivated a close relationship with North Korea on ballistic missile programs, beginning with the acquisition of Scud missiles in North Korea back in the 1980s. Iran continues to pursue capabilities that could ultimately be used to build missile-deliverable nuclear weapons, and missile sales and missile test information have been a key source of hard currency for the Kim regime.

In the past decade, Iran and North Korea have also cooperated on nuclear research and technology. In 2015 alone, North Korea nuclear experts allegedly visited Iran at least three times to exchange information and intelligence.

Secretary of Defense Ash Carter stated in April that North Korea and Iran could be cooperating to develop a nuclear weapon, including sharing technology related to nuclear weapons, material production, or data from nuclear or explosives testing.

Desperately insecure and cash-starved, North Korea remains hell bent on developing and improving its nuclear capabilities. With Iran's impending access to $100 billion of frozen assets under the Joint Comprehensive Plan of Action, Iran could use some of those assets to procure material, technologies, and expertise from North Korea. I hope our witnesses can inform us about whether this should be a major concern for Congress.

Given the history of cooperation between North Korea and Iran, I am very concerned about what the Iran deal may mean for our national security interests in both the Middle East and Asia. We need to know their motives and the implications of their cooperation so we can prevent bad deals from the start and not allow bad actors to unite in nuclear proliferation efforts against international agreements.

Thank you, Mr. Chairman. I yield back.

Mr. POE. I thank the gentleman from Arizona.

The Chair recognizes the ranking member for the Asia and Pacific Subcommittee, Mr. Sherman from California.

Mr. SHERMAN. I will use my 5 minutes to focus on our hearing this morning.

Secretary Kerry, I think, gave us some very interesting information, as he said that whether this deal holds or doesn't hold, we are free to impose new sanctions on Iran to try to change its behavior with regard to terrorism, with regard to holding four American hostages, and with regard to its complicity in the crimes of Assad in Syria.

Deal or no deal, we need to adopt additional sanctions. And the work, every time we have adopted sanctions on Iran, has started in this room. And I look forward to working, deal or no deal, with everyone here to have the sanctions that will change Iranian behavior.

I point out that the proponents of the deal say sanctions changed Iran's behavior and caused it to give up its nuclear weapon design, what the proponents say is an excellent deal. The opponents of the deal say sanctions can change Iran's behavior if we only stick to our guns and get tougher. So the one thing everybody that has come to this room seems to agree on is that sanctions can change Iran's behavior, and that outside the nuclear area, Iran's behavior needs a lot of changing.

The second comment that Senator Kerry made in response to one of my questions is that, as everyone knows, if we override the President's veto, certain U.S. statutory sanctions legally are the law of the land and the waiver provisions don't exist, so the President is obligated by law to enforce them. But I have been at this for a long time, and we know that Presidents, though, don't always enforce statutes against Iran. In fact, the Iran Sanctions Act was not enforced once by the prior administration, and a lot of sanctions were pretty much ignored the first couple of years at least of this administration.

And I asked the Secretary whether he would obey the law under those circumstances, and he said that that was too hypothetical a question. I would like to go on record to say that under all hypothetical circumstances, I intend to obey the law, but moreover, the Secretary came to us to talk about a hypothetical situation: What happens if Congress overrides the veto? And he told us what India would do, what Europe would do, what Iran would do, what China would do, but when I asked him what the administration would do under those circumstances, it was too hypothetical.

As to the issue before us, Iran's going to have a lot of money; North Korea has nuclear weapons and a thirst for money. What could go wrong? As we know, obviously, North Korea could sell a completed nuclear weapon. They could sell fissile material. They could sell a weaponization plan. They could sell a bomb without the fissile material and any combination of this. Iran and North Korea have a long relationship of working on military matters together from the 1980s, which increased in the 1990s. We used to get annual reports until 2013 of the concern that North Korea would export its nuclear technology.

So we don't have any proof that it is about to happen. We don't have any proof that it has already happened. We just have a country that has almost seemingly a desperate desire for nuclear weapons and another one with a desperate desire for money. And we know that the one with the desperate desire for nuclear weapons is going to get its hands on a lot of money very soon.

Now, the question is what we do about it. We have got to look at planes and ships that would connect the two. I think if there is an exchange of money for nuclear material, it is much more likely to take place on a plane. A ship gives us a chance to track it and a chance to make a decision as to whether to interdict and board. Of course, a ship is also possible. We should not be encouraging the civil aviation of Iran by selling them planes and parts. We know they are going to use those planes to take thugs to Damascus to kill people. And we hope they don't use the planes to go pick up a nuclear weapon in North Korea.

So we have got to see what are the opportunities to interdict either the shipment of a bomb in one direction or cash in the other. We have got to keep track of what Iran does with the $56 billion to $150 billion they get from this deal. But, finally, I think we are dependent upon China, which exercises such significant control over the most critical aspects of what the North Korean Government does. If China is willing to turn a blind eye to a cash-for-bomb situation, I don't know if we can stop it, and we certainly— if they were willing to turn that blind eye at Beijing Airport, I know we couldn't stop it.

I yield back.

Mr. POE. Thank the gentleman.

The Chair recognizes the right honorable gentlewoman from the Middle East and North Africa Subcommittee, Ms. Ileana Ros-Lehtinen from Florida.

Ms. ROS-LEHTINEN. Well, thank you so much, Judge Poe.

I want to thank Judge Poe and Chairman Salmon for bringing our three subcommittees together to focus on the nexus between these two rogue regimes, Iran and North Korea.

As Congress continues to do our due diligence on the Joint Comprehensive Plan of Action between the P5+1 and Iran that the Obama administration submitted to us last week, it is important that we do not make the same mistakes again.

In 2008, I was outspoken against the George W. Bush administration for removing North Korea from the State Sponsors of Terrorism list as a concession to Pyongyang during negotiations over its nuclear program. And I am also outspoken against this administration's concessions to Tehran during the negotiations and ultimately this deal.

Yet as far back as the Clinton administration, each administration continues to make the same mistakes of offering these rogue nations concessions while allowing them to maintain their nuclear infrastructure and misguidedly falling back on hope that this time will be different, this time things will change.

These negotiations mirror the same track that the nuclear negotiations with North Korea took. Iran has been following the North Korean playbook on exactly how to extract concessions from the U.S. and the international community while simultaneously continuing to improve its nuclear program, expand its infrastructure, and support continues for its illicit activities.

But it isn't just that the Iranian regime is following the North Korean playbook, successfully, I might add, it is that the Obama administration is following the same failed playbook that the Clinton and Bush administrations pursued. It is alarming and striking just how similar the language is between President Clinton's 1994 announcement of a nuclear agreement with North Korea and President Obama's announcement of a nuclear agreement with Iran earlier this month. Last week, Alan Dershowitz wrote about the similarities and even posted a chart that represented the similarities in the language, the words used between the Clinton administration and the Obama statements.

In 1994, President Clinton said that the North Korea agreement will make the U.S., the Korean Peninsula, and the world safer. He assured us that the deal didn't rely on trust, that compliance would be certified by the IAEA. President Clinton also made the dubious claim that because of our willingness to engage North Korea on its nuclear profile, that would be a crucial step toward drawing Pyongyang into the global community and predicted the end of the rogue regime's isolation.

Does any of this sound familiar to us? It should, because these are the same arguments that President Obama used when announcing the deal and that were used today in our Foreign Affairs full committee hearing.

When the North Korea deal was reached, one of the most significant flaws was that it failed to dismantle any of Pyongyang's nuclear infrastructure. The deal was designed merely to delay the North Korean bomb, not prevent it, and we even promised, as we are doing in the JCPoA, to modernize and improve North Korea's nuclear infrastructure.

And now we are aiming to prevent the Iranian bomb. The totality of this deal hinges on the bet by the administration and the rest of the P5+1 that the Iranian regime will see the error of its ways and wants to be part of the global community and will forsake its support for terror and other illicit behavior. That is a heck of a gamble to make when all of, not even just a preponderance, but all of the evidence indicates that this is not the likely outcome, but rather that Iran will use this as a means to increase its belligerence. And now with this deal, we are likely to see an increase in Iran-North Korea activity on ballistic missiles and covert nuclear actions because not only will we be lifting the sanctions on Iranian scientists and on Iran's nuclear program, but we will be lifting the sanctions on its ballistic missile program and its military leaders. And that is where Iran and North Korea are likely to resume their cooperation, on the weaponization and the ballistic missiles.

This is a dangerous gamble for us to make with U.S. national security, and it is not a gamble that I or any of us should be willing to take. That is why we must reject this deal, demand a better deal, or else reimpose the sanctions and use the only action that Iran understands, strength, to force it to abandon its nuclear ambitions.

Thank you, Mr. Chairman.

Mr. POE. The gentlelady yields back.

The Chair will recognize the gentleman from Virginia, Mr. Connolly, for 1 minute.

Mr. CONNOLLY. Thank you, Mr. Chairman.

You know, I just heard my friend from Florida equate these two agreements and call for the vote to disapprove the pending agreement with Iran. I think there are some lessons from North Korea. One was we decided consciously to not engage, and we paid a very heavy price for that. And in the case of Iran, we have decided to engage, and we have an agreement that you couldn't possibly compare to that with North Korea. And I just think, you know, we should never be afraid to be engaged, especially when it comes to the nuclear question. I don't think it is so cut and dried.

While I respect my friend from Florida, I also respectfully disagree. I don't think this is a clear-cut case at all that calls for absolute rejection and renunciation by the Congress of the United States. I think that is a very momentous step, not a political one, it shouldn't be a political one and one we ought to contemplate with great care.

So I certainly look forward to the testimony today, and I would like to hear some of the differences between North Korea and Iran, because I happen to think they are pretty profound.

I yield back.

Mr. POE. Thank the gentleman from Virginia.

The Chair recognizes the gentleman from South Carolina, Mr. Duncan.

Mr. DUNCAN. Thank you, Mr. Chairman. I have got a question for the ranking member. You know, what is keeping North Korea from selling ballistic missiles or nuclear weapons to Iran today? Regardless of whether we walk away from this agreement or not, North Korea can still sell them the weapons. Nothing is stopping them.

In February and April 2007, North Korea agreed to "abandoning all nuclear weapons and existing nuclear programs, and returning at an earlier date to the Treaty on the Nonproliferation of Nuclear Weapons and the IAEA safeguards." Supposedly this significant achievement commits all six parties to a denuclearized Korean Peninsula and will lead to a more stable and secure northeast Asia. For doing this, North Korea received, as it complies with its commitment, they received 950,000 tons of heavy fuel oil. Well, guess what? In September 2008, they cranked the nuclear program back up, and to this day, they have a nuclear weapon. Those are the facts. North Korea has got a nuclear weapon.

If Iran wants a nuclear weapon, regardless of what this agreement that we talked about today at length, if we don't have the ability to inspect the appropriate sites, they are still going to get a nuclear weapon. This agreement has no teeth, and they are going to have $150 billion to give arms and money to Hezbollah and Hamas. They are still exporters of terrorism. Those are the facts.

I yield back.

Mr. POE. The gentleman yields back.

Does any other member wish to be recognized for an opening statement? If not, I will introduce our witnesses.

Once again, I want to thank all four of you for being here today on this day of Iran at the Capitol Hill.

Mr. Ilan Berman is vice president of the American Foreign Policy Council. Mr. Berman is widely published on issues of regional security and foreign policy and has also consulted for the CIA, the Department of Defense, and many other government agencies.

Ms. Claudia Rosett is a journalist-in-residence at the Foundation for Defense of Democracies. Ms. Rosett is widely recognized as a groundbreaking reporter and won the 2005 Eric Breindel award and the Mightier Pen award for her work on the U.N. Oil-for-Food scandal.

Dr. Larry Niksch is a senior associate at the Center for Strategic and International Studies. Dr. Niksch specializes in U.S. security policy in East Asia and the Western Pacific.

And Dr. Jim Walsh is a research associate at the Massachusetts Institute of Technology's Security Studies Program. Dr. Walsh is one of a handful, and a very few handful, of Americans who have traveled both to Iran and North Korea for talks with officials regarding nuclear issues.

Each of you will have 5 minutes. There should be three lights in front of you. The red one means it is time to stop.

We will start with Mr. Berman. You have 5 minutes. And your statements all are in the record, so we have all your statements. You may summarize them or you may read your statement.

STATEMENT OF MR. ILAN BERMAN, VICE PRESIDENT, AMERICAN FOREIGN POLICY COUNCIL

Mr. BERMAN. Thank you, sir.

Chairman Poe, Chairman Salmon, Chairwoman Ros-Lehtinen, Ranking Members Keating, Sherman, and Deutch, thank you so much for the opportunity to be present before you today to talk about this issue.

The strategic partnership between Iran and North Korea is one of the most significant, yet one of the most often overlooked aspects of the strategic threat that is posed both by Iran and by North Korea. It is also one that today, as Congress begins to deliberate over the new nuclear agreement struck between the P5+1 and Iran, merits renewed attention by this committee and by Capitol Hill as a whole.

Because my time is limited here, let me focus on just three aspects of this strategic relationship, which are important in their own right, certainly, but also important in particular because of the implications they hold for the JCPoA.

The first is that Iran's relationship with North Korea is vibrant, certainly, but it is not unique. It makes up part of a larger global strategy that is being pursued by the Islamic Republic, and not just in Asia: It is being pursued in Latin America; it is being pursued in Europe; it is being pursued in Africa. And it is one that is designed simultaneously to lessen Iran's global isolation as a result of the sanctions imposed by us and our international partners, and also, more ambitiously, to expand its strategic reach. And in Asia, in particular, what Iran has done has mirrored very much the Obama administration's own Asia pivot, where in 2011, we have declared our interest in the region as an area of new opportunity and new strategic focus. The Iranians have done so as well, but not just in an economic sense and not just in a military sense. Iran has looked toward Asia in particular as a defense industrial hot spot. And in this regard, the partnership Iran has built with North Korea is of particular importance.

The second takeaway is that North Korea has materially aided Iran's strategic capabilities, and as a result, it has expanded the threat that Iran poses to the West. The members all talked in their opening statements about ballistic missile and nuclear cooperation between Iran and North Korea. This is vibrant. It is ongoing. And there is credible evidence to suggest that cooperation on these fronts has helped to materially enhance not only the Iranian nuclear program, but also the sophistication and the know-how of the North Korean effort as well. I am happy to delve deeper into that in the question and answers.

The third takeaway, and I think the most germane, given that today is Iran day on Capitol Hill, is that Iran has learned a tremendous amount about nuclear diplomacy and about the way the West negotiates through the North Korean experience. Since the early 1990s, North Korea has engaged in extensive diplomacy with the international community over its nuclear program, and it has obtained significant diplomatic and economic inducements as a result of purported good behavior. These inducements have played an instrumental role in strengthening and stabilizing the Kim regime in Pyongyang, but they have not led Pyongyang to give up its nuclear program. To the contrary, it is very credible to say that they have made it possible for the North Koreans to continue their nuclear program and strategic programs.

The North Koreans have reneged over time on every single one of the commitments that they have given in the Agreed Framework as well as in the now defunct Six Party Talks that stretched from 2003 to 2009. They have done so, notably, without adverse consequences, because the international community continues to maintain that a conciliatory posture rather than a punitive posture is likely to change North Korean behavior.

Here we come to Iran, because Iran today finds itself in very much the same position. In fact, I would make the case that Iran finds itself in a much better one because the scope of the financial relief that is inherent in the JCPoA dwarfs the kind of economic and political stimuli that North Korea received as a result of its previous negotiations with the West.

I made this case in a hearing last week, and just to reiterate, because the historical evidence backs it up, the JCPoA is tantamount to a Marshall Plan for the Islamic Republic of Iran. This sounds like an exaggeration, but it isn't. By way of comparison, I will point out that, under the terms of the JCPoA, later this year or early in 2016, once we have requisite verification from the IAEA, the U.S. will begin unblocking $100 billion to $150 billion of frozen Iranian oil revenue. That sum equates to roughly a quarter of Iran's annual gross domestic product, which last year was $415 billion. It also matches or exceeds the entire post-World War II reconstruction plan for Europe that was marshaled by the Truman administration. That effort was launched in 1948 and facilitated the disbursement of $13 billion, equivalent to $120 billion in today's currency, to 17 separate countries in Southern and Eastern Europe over the course of 4 years.

Now, we hope that Iran will use the financial windfall that it receives from the JCPoA for domestic purposes. But it is quite clear that they can use it just as easily, because money is fungible, on strategic capabilities, on the support of terrorism. If and when they do so, and I think there is every reason to believe that they will, they will find, in their partnership with North Korea, a cash-strapped partner that is more than willing to provide them with the resources that will materially expand both their ballistic missile program and their nuclear program.

Thank you.
[The prepared statement of Mr. Berman follows:]

The Iran-North Korea Strategic Alliance

Testimony before the
House Committee on Foreign Affairs
Subcommittee on Terrorism, Nonproliferation, and Trade
Subcommittee on Asia and the Pacific
Subcommittee on the Middle East and North Africa

Ilan Berman
Vice President
American Foreign Policy Council

July 28, 2015

Chairman Poe, Chairman Salmon, Chairwoman Ros-Lehtinen, Ranking Members Keating, Sherman and Deutch, and distinguished members of the Subcommittees:

Thank you for the opportunity to appear before you today to discuss the strategic partnership between the Islamic Republic of Iran and the Democratic People's Republic of Korea. That alliance represents one of the most significant, yet overlooked, dimensions of the contemporary challenge posed by both countries. And today, as Congress deliberates the new nuclear agreement struck between Iran and the P5+1, it is a topic that merits renewed attention.

IRAN'S ASIA PIVOT

On January 26, 2012, Defense Secretary Leon Panetta and Joint Chiefs Chairman Gen. Martin Dempsey convened a major press conference at the Pentagon to outline the policies and programs that had been prioritized by the Defense Department in order to build a "smaller and leaner, but agile, flexible, ready and technologically advanced" military.[1] The centerpiece of the event was the unveiling of a new strategic priority: a "rebalancing" of American resources and attention to Asia.

"U.S. economic and security interests are inextricably linked to developments in the arc extending from the Western Pacific and East Asia into the Indian Ocean region and South Asia, creating a mix of evolving challenges and opportunities," the supporting policy planning document outlined. "Accordingly, while the U.S. military will continue to contribute to security globally, we will of necessity rebalance toward the Asia-Pacific region."[2]

The rationale behind the move was both practical and opportunistic. Politically, the preceding three years had been difficult ones for the Obama administration in the Middle East, punctuated by the turmoil of the "Arab Spring," the outbreak of the Syrian civil war, and numerous other crises for which the White House did not seem to have a ready response. Against this backdrop, a "pivot" to Asia was widely seen as a quest for greener foreign policy pastures. Practically, meanwhile, the Administration sought to exploit the widespread uneasiness generated by China's so-called "peaceful" rise to regional prominence, which had precipitated a growing willingness among Asian nations to partner more fully with Washington on security and political issues.

The United States has not been unique in this regard, however. A number of other foreign nations have mirrored this eastward tilt, turning toward Asia as an arena of economic opportunity and strategic engagement. Iran has been prominent among them, and its turn toward Asia represents an important part of a larger "peripheral strategy" by which the Islamic Republic has sought both to ease its international isolation and, more recently, to expand its strategic reach and global influence.

Economically, regional partners such as China have provided the Islamic Republic with a lifeline that has helped to significantly lessen the economic pain caused by American and European sanctions. As of 2013, China alone accounted for approximately 50 percent of Iran's total crude oil exports (roughly 500,000 barrels per day).[3] Today, that figure is larger still; as part of its confidence-building measures toward Tehran, the Obama administration has suspended implementation of the 2010 *Comprehensive Iran Sanctions, Accountability and Divestment Act*, which requires major Iranian energy clients to steadily draw down their imports of crude from the Islamic Republic in order to avoid sanctions from the United States.[4] Predictably, energy ties between the two countries have surged as a result. In the first half of 2014, for example, China imported some 50 percent more oil from Iran than the same period a year earlier.[5] The situation remains largely the same today.[6]

Moreover, the region has emerged as a significant illicit hub for Iran's clerical army, the Islamic Revolutionary Guard Corps (IRGC). In May of 2014, Asian news sources disclosed a web of suspicious financial activity throughout the region, encompassing more than $1 billion of funds squirreled away in a major South Korean bank by Petrosina Arya, an IRGC-linked company, and active accounts by branches of Khatam al-Anbiya, the IRGC's construction headquarters, in Malaysia.[7] The financial activity, news reports concluded, were part of a systematic effort by the Iranian regime aimed at "dodging internationally coordinated economic sanctions."[8]

Strategically, meanwhile, Asia has become a significant covert theater for the Islamic Republic. Over the past several years, operatives of Iran's chief terrorist proxy, Hezbollah, have attempted to perpetrate acts of terror throughout the region, including in Thailand and the Philippines.[9] On at least one occasion, in February 2012, Iranian-linked radicals successfully bombed an Israeli diplomatic vehicle in New Delhi, India.[10]

Equally significant, however, is Asia's position as a hub for defense technology, including critical assistance to Iran's ballistic missile and nuclear programs. It is in this context that North Korea has emerged as what is arguably Iran's most important regional ally.

A VIBRANT PARTNERSHIP

In North Korea's capitol of Pyongyang, the embassy of the Islamic Republic of Iran holds particular pride of place. It occupies a sprawling, seven building compound complete with a mosque that is the first in North Korea, and one of only five places of worship formally allowed in the city.[11] The compound is a tangible manifestation of the close ties that have developed between Tehran and Pyongyang over the past three decades.

That partnership finds its roots in the immediate aftermath of the 1979 Islamic Revolution when, in order to evade the weapons embargo imposed by the Carter administration, the IRGC began to erect an indigenous weapons infrastructure. In pursuit of this goal, Iran procured arms from a number of foreign states, most prominently China and the USSR. But Kim Il-Sung's North Korea figured significantly as well; by the early 1980s, the U.S. government estimated that China and North Korea cumulatively were providing the Islamic Republic with 40 percent of its arms. By the late 1980s, that figure had risen to 70 percent.[12]

The centerpiece of the budding Iran-North Korea relationship quickly became collaboration on strategic capabilities. The two countries are said to have launched cooperative missile development back in 1985 under an agreement through which Iran helped to underwrite North Korea's production of 300 kilometer-range Scud-B missiles in exchange for new technology, as well as the option to purchase the completed Scuds. Iran exercised that option two years later, when it reportedly purchased 100 Scud-Bs for use in the closing battles of its long-running war with Iraq.[13]

This interaction expanded in the 1990s, when Iran and North Korea began joint development of Iran's *Shahab* missile series, which – not coincidentally – is closely based on North Korea's nuclear-capable *No Dong* medium range missile. Indeed, according to ballistic missile experts, the *No Dong* and the longer-range *Taepo Dong-1*, and *Taepodong-2* missiles were the basis for Iran's *Shahab 3* and *Shahab 4*, now in service, and its *Shahab 5* and *6* variants, currently in development. The two states are now thought to be collaborating on the development of a nuclear-capable intercontinental ballistic missile.[14]

The Islamic Republic has also relied on the DPRK for help with its nuclear program. A January 2006 article in *Jane's Defense Weekly*, for example, noted that the IRGC had initiated procurement contracts with North Korea to bolster fortifications for nuclear facilities in anticipation of possible preemptive strikes. As part of this effort, a group affiliated with the North Korean government was involved in tunneling and designing underground construction around the Isfahan and Natanz sites.[15]

It is not surprising, therefore, that Iran and North Korea's strategic capabilities have evolved in parallel – and via extensive collaboration. Iranian scientists and technicians, for example, have had a front-row seat to the DPRK's ballistic missile development, regularly attending its missile launches since at least the early 1990s. That cooperation, moreover, is still underway. Iran is known to have dispatched delegations to attend North Korean flight tests of the *No-dong* in July of 2006 and March of 2009.[16] And in the Fall of 2013, the *Washington Free Beacon* reported that a delegation of Iranian technical experts had recently visited Pyongyang as part of ongoing collaboration on the development of a new rocket booster; technology that could significantly advance Iran's long-range missile effort. U.S. intelligence sources cited by the paper described the 80-ton booster in question as a potential thruster for a "super ICBM" or a "heavy lift space launcher" – in other words, something that could allow Iran, currently a regional missile power, to become a global one.[17]

Compelling evidence also exists that Pyongyang and Tehran have collaborated on the nuclear front. During the early 1990s, much of that interaction was mostly secret, due to U.S. pressure on North Korea over its own nuclear development. Even so, press reports at the time strongly suggested that some level of cooperation was indeed underway.[18] Thereafter, cooperation became more active – and public. Both countries, for example, are known to have benefited from the nuclear know-how of Pakistani scientist AQ Khan and his proliferation network, and North Korea is said to have dispatched hundreds of nuclear experts to work in the Islamic Republic and provided it with key nuclear software.[19] And during North Korea's February 2013 nuclear test, a delegation of Iranian scientists (who had offered to pay tens of millions of dollars for access) was in attendance.[20] All of this has led Western experts to speculate that North Korea may have served as an atomic proxy for the Islamic Republic – and that one or more of the nuclear tests carried out by the DPRK over the past decade was in fact done to test Iranian capabilities.[21]

North Korea's partnership with Iran also extends to support of Iran's terror proxy of choice: Lebanon's Hezbollah militia. Several top Hezbollah officials are known to have received military training in North Korea, among them the group's secretary general, Hassan Nasrallah, Hezbollah intelligence and security chief Ibrahim Akil, and Mustapha Badreddine, its counter-espionage czar.[22] The DPRK is also believed to have aided Hezbollah with the construction of elaborate underground tunnels in southern Lebanon – passageways that were uncovered in the aftermath of the group's 2006 war with Israel.[23]

Moreover, other rogues have benefited from the Iranian-DPRK alliance as well, chief among them the regime of Bashar al-Assad in Syria. According to a high-level Iranian defector, Ali Reza Asghari, Iran has helped to finance North Korea's participation in Syria's nuclear weapons program.[24] This allegation is lent credence by the fact that Syria's al-Khibar nuclear reactor, which was successfully destroyed by Israel in a covert bombing campaign in 2007, turned out to be of a design analogous to the DPRK's own nuclear plant at Yongbyon.[25]

The extent of the strategic bonds between the two countries was demonstrated in September 2012, when Iran and North Korea inked a pact on scientific-technical cooperation.[26] The agreement, which closely resembles a similar arrangement signed between the North Koreans and Syria roughly a decade earlier, was presided over by Iranian president Mahmoud Ahmadinejad and Kim Yong Nam, the powerful Chairman of the Presidium of North Korea's Supreme People's Assembly, in a concrete sign of the importance that the two countries place on their "fraternal" ties. But it was also much more. "The Islamic Republic of Iran and North Korea have common enemies since the arrogant powers can't bear independent governments," Iran's Supreme Leader, Ali Khamenei, is said to have told Kim during his visit.[27]

Khamenei's message was unmistakable: Iran sees North Korea as a partner nation, and as an ally in its efforts to increase its own global power and influence, and dilute that of the West.

IRAN'S LESSONS LEARNED

The partnership forged between North Korea and Iran over the past three decades has yielded significant benefits for both countries. Through it, the DPRK has become an important stakeholder in Iran's development of ballistic missile and nuclear technology, and its own capabilities in turn can be presumed to have benefited materially from Iran's assistance and input. At the same time, North Korean assistance has significantly accelerated Iran's strategic programs and made them a truly multilateral affair.

Today, amid the deliberations taking place on Capitol Hill over the new nuclear agreement negotiated between Iran and the P5+1, this relationship has taken on added significance, for several reasons.

North Korea provides Iran with a successful "model" for nuclear diplomacy. Since the early 1990s, North Korea has engaged in extensive diplomacy with the international community over its atomic effort, obtaining significant diplomatic and economic benefits as a result. Inducements provided to the DPRK as a result of the 1994 "Agreed Framework" and subsequently the now-defunct Six-Party Talks (which stretched from 2003 until 2009) played an instrumental role in strengthening and stabilizing the regime in Pyongyang. They did not, however, lead Pyongyang to give up its nuclear program. Over time, the North Korean regime has reneged on every single one of its international commitments relating to its nuclear effort, from uranium enrichment to plutonium production to atomic testing.[28] It has done so, moreover, largely without consequence from the international community, which has consistently attempted to moderate North Korean conduct through conciliatory rather than punitive measures.

Iran now finds itself in much the same position. Already, nuclear discussions with the P5+1 have netted Iran the possibility of extensive near-term sanctions relief (valued at $100 billion or more), as well as exceedingly favorable technical terms that preserve and perfect – rather than roll back – its nuclear project. Much like North Korea before it, the Iranian regime can be expected to pocket these concessions as a means of strengthening its economic position and consolidating its domestic power. But, like North Korea, the West's current diplomacy is not likely to chill Tehran's enthusiasm for nuclear status. To the contrary, if history is any indication, Iran will follow North Korea's example and leverage its nuclear advances to garner still greater concessions from the international community in the future.

North Korea is a potential source of illicit technology for Iran. In its terms and provisions, the JCPOA is overwhelmingly focused on the overt means by which the Islamic Republic might attain nuclear status. However, the agreement is largely silent on the covert methods by which it could do so. Thus, even though President Obama has maintained that the deal closes off "all pathways" by which Iran might attain a nuclear capability in the coming decade, experts have warned that a clandestine "pathway" to nuclearization, involving covert procurement of materiel from foreign suppliers, in fact still remains open.[29]

The nature of ties between Tehran and Pyongyang suggest that North Korea could be one of the key sources of covertly-acquired nuclear materiel for the Islamic Republic, should Iran's leaders choose to develop a capability in this fashion. Indeed, in his January 2014 testimony before the Senate Select Committee on Intelligence, Director of National Intelligence James Clapper made note of "North Korea's export of ballistic missiles and associated materials to several countries, including Iran and Syria."[30] The United States has not resolutely confronted this illicit commerce to date. To the contrary, the Obama administration – in its eagerness to conclude a nuclear agreement with Iran – has turned a blind eye to instances of Iranian-North Korean proliferation in the recent past.[31] And because it has, North Korea currently represents an alternative pathway to the atomic bomb for Iran—one that would allow the Islamic Republic to go nuclear over the next decade, even with a diplomatic deal in place. (Moreover, because the JCPOA is silent on the question of Iranian ballistic missile capabilities, Iranian-North Korean commerce in this arena likewise can be expected to continue unimpeded.)

North Korea has demonstrated the benefits of covert nuclearization. President Obama and his advisors have repeatedly intoned that "all options," including military action, remain on the table for dealing with Iran, should the current nuclear pact break down. U.S. policy toward North Korea over the past decade-and-a-half, however, demonstrates that this is not the case. Rather, North Korea's unexpected disclosure to the Bush administration in the Fall of 2002 that it possessed a nascent nuclear capability helped to stymie U.S. policy in Asia, which until then had included a range of policy options (among them the use of force against North Korean nuclear facilities), and nudged America and its diplomatic partners into the ultimately futile Six Party Talks.

In much the same way, Iran's leadership understands that the maturity of its nuclear effort will help ensure regime stability and limit Western options. By this metric, the terms of the JCPOA represent a resounding strategic victory for the Iranian regime. At the outset of those negotiations, the objective of the Administration was to obtain a "freeze for freeze," under which Iran would agree to halt its uranium enrichment activities in exchange for a lifting of sanctions. In response to Iranian objections, this goal was downgraded to the more modest one of "freeze for transparency": sanctions relief in exchange for comprehensive Western oversight of Iran's nuclear facilities. But the final terms contained in the JCPOA do not even meet this standard; rather, pursuant to a number of key provisions – including Russian cooperation on nuclear research at the Fordow Fuel Enrichment Plant (Annex I, Section H), European aid in strengthening Iranian nuclear security (Annex III, Section D), and international assistance in aiding Iran to master the nuclear fuel cycle through fuel fabrication (Annex IV, Section 2) – the P5+1 powers will actually help to improve the capability and sophistication of Iran's nuclear effort over time. As a result, they will bring Iran closer to a baseline nuclear capability over the coming decade, perhaps considerably so. In the process, they will greatly constrain U.S. options for responding to Iran's nuclear program, either during the time the JCPOA is in force or the period that immediately follows.

That Iran has successfully learned these lessons is a testament to our failed nuclear diplomacy with North Korea over the past two decades. That Iran is now in a position to act upon them reflects the deficiencies of our new nuclear bargain with the Islamic Republic.

---

[1] Colin Clark, "JSF Survives, Global Hawk Dies, Global Strike Revives; Panetta's Budget," *Breaking Defense*, January 26, 2012, http://breakingdefense.com/2012/01/jsf-survives-global-hawk-dies-global-strike-revives-panetta-r/.

[2] U.S. Department of Defense, Office of the Secretary of Defense, *Sustaining U.S. Global Leadership: Priorities for 21st Century Defense*, January 2012, "www.defense.gov/news/Defense_Strategic_Guidance.pdf.

[3] As cited in Zachary Keck, "Asia is Purchasing Nearly All of Iran's Oil," *The Diplomat*, January 5, 2013, http://thediplomat.com/2013/01/asia-is-purchasing-nearly-all-of-irans-oil/.

[4] *Comprehensive Iran Sanctions, Accountability, and Divestment Act of 2010*, Public Law 11-195, July 1, 2010, http://www.treasury.gov/resource-center/sanctions/Documents/hr2194.pdf.

[5] Wayne Ma, "China Imports Record Amount of Iranian Crude," *Wall Street Journal*, July 21, 2014, http://online.wsj.com/articles/china-imports-record-amount-of-iranian-crude-1405946504.

[6] "China's Iran Oil Imports Hit 2-Mth High in June – Customs," Reuters, July 21, 2015, https://en-maktoob.news.yahoo.com/chinas-iran-oil-imports-hit-2-mth-high-084053906--business.html.

[7] "Iran Elite Group Suspected of Keeping Secret Funds in Asia," Kyodo News, May 4, 2014, http://www.globalpost.com/dispatch/news/kyodo-news-international/140504/iran-elite-group-suspected-keeping-secret-funds-asia.

[8] Ibid.

[9] See Haroon Siddique and agencies, "Thailand Arrests Hezbollah Suspect After Terror Tipoff," *Guardian* (London), January 13, 2012, http://www.theguardian.com/world/2012/jan/13/thailand-arrests-hezbollah-suspect-terror-tipoff; See, for example, "Hezbollah Planned to Attack Israeli Tourists," *Daily Star* (Lebanon), April 19, 2014, http://www.dailystar.com.lb/News/Lebanon-News/2014/Apr-19/253847-hezbollah-planned-to-attack-israeli-tourists.ashx.

[10] Joel Greenberg and Simon Denyer, "Israel Blames Iran for India and Georgia Bombings; Tehran Denies Role," *Washington Post*, February 13, 2012, http://www.washingtonpost.com/world/bombs-target-israeli-diplomats-in-india-georgia-2-injured/2012/02/13/gIQA2kDIAR_story.html.

[11] Chad O'Carroll, "Iran Builds Pyongyang's First Mosque," *NKNews*, January 22, 2013. http://www.nknews.org/2013/01/iran-buillds-pyongyangs-first-mosque/.

[12] Christina Y. Lin, "China, Iran, and North Korea: A Triangular Strategic Alliance," *Middle East Review of International Affairs* 14, no. 1, March 2010, http://www.gloria-center.org/2010/03/lin-2010-03-05/.

[13] Ibid.

[14] Ibidem.

[15] Mark E. Manyin. *North Korea: Back on the Terrorism List?* Congressional Research Service, June 29, 2010, http://www.fas.org/sgp/crs/row/RL30613.pdf

[16] See Stephanie Griffith, "Iran Present at North Korean Missile Launch Says U.S.," Agence France Presse, July 20, 2006, http://www.spacewar.com/reports/Iran_Present_At_North_Korea_Missile_Launch_Says_US_999.html; See also "Reports: Iran Experts Aiding North Korea Rocket Launch," *Fox News*, March 29, 2009, http://www.foxnews.com/story/2009/03/29/reports-iran-experts-aiding-north-korea-rocket-launch/.

[17] Bill Gertz, "Iran, North Korea Secretly Developing New Long-Range Rocket Booster for ICBMs," *Washington Free Beacon*, November 26, 2013, http://freebeacon.com/national-security/iran-north-korea-secretly-developing-new-long-range-rocket-booster-for-icbms/.

[18] See "Secret Nuclear Sites Detailed," *Iran Brief*, November 6, 1995.

[19] "Source: Hundreds of NK Nuclear and Missile Experts Working in Iran," *Korea Times* (Seoul), November 13, 2011, http://www.koreatimes.co.kr/www/news/nation/2011/11/113_98613.html; Madeline Chambers, "North Korea Supplied Nuclear Software to Iran: German Report," Reuters, August 24, 2011, http://www.reuters.com/article/2011/08/24/us-nuclear-northkorea-iran-idUSTRE77N2FZ20110824.

[20] "Iran 'Paid Millions for Ringside Seat at N. Korean Nuke Test,'" *Chosun Ilbo* (Seoul), February 18, 2013, http://english.chosun.com/site/data/html_dir/2013/02/18/2013021801176.html.

[21] See, for example, David P. Goldman, "Did Iran Test a Nuclear Bomb in North Korea in 2010?" *PJ Media*, March 4, 2012, http://pjmedia.com/spengler/2012/03/04/did-iran-test-a-nuclear-bomb-in-north-korea-in-2010/.

[22] Ileana Ros-Lehtinen, "North Korea's Support for Terrorist Groups and State Sponsors of Terrorism," internal memo to House Republicans. May 8, 2008, http://freekorea.us/2008/05/09/leaked-to-ofk-internal-house-memo-on-n-koreas-support-for-terrorism/.

[23] Victor Cha and Gabriel Scheinmann, "North Korea's Hamas Connection: 'Below' the Surface?" *The National Interest*, September 4, 2014, http://nationalinterest.org/feature/north-koreas-hamas-connection-below-the-surface-11195.

[24] "Iranian Defector Tipped Syrian Nuke Plans," Associated Press, March 19, 2009, http://www.ynetnews.com/articles/0,7340,L-3689320,00.html.

[25] Robin Wright and Joby Warrick, "Syrians Disassembling Ruins at Site Bombed by Israel, Officials Say," *Washington Post*, October 19, 2007.

[26] Jay Solomon, "Iran-North Korea Pact Draws Concern," *Wall Street Journal*, March 8, 2013, http://online.wsj.com/news/articles/SB10001424127887323628804578348640295282274.

[27] Ibid.

[28] Claudia Rosett, "Iran Follows in North Korea's Nuclear Shoes," *Asian Wall Street Journal*, November 19, 2013, http://online.wsj.com/news/articles/SB10001424052702304439804579207422182734460.

[29] Orde F. Kittrie, "The China-Iran Nuclear Pipeline: How to Shut it Down," *Foreign Affairs*, July 13, 2015, https://www.foreignaffairs.com/articles/china/2015-07-13/china-iran-nuclear-pipeline.

[30] James R. Clapper, Statement for the Record before the Senate Select Committee on Intelligence, January 29, 2014, http://www.dni.gov/files/documents/Intelligence%20Reports/2014%20WWTA%20%20SFR_SSCI_29_Jan.pdf.

[31] See, for example, Bill Gertz, "North Korea Transfers Missile Goods to Iran During Nuclear Talks," *Washington Free Beacon*, April 15, 2015, http://freebeacon.com/national-security/north-korea-transfers-missile-goods-to-iran-during-nuclear-talks/.

Mr. POE. Thank you, Mr. Berman.

I would like to remind witnesses and members to abide by the 5-minute rule. We have votes in an hour and 5 minutes. Hopefully we can finish this hearing before we have votes. If not, then we will all get to come back later tonight and finish the hearing.

Ms. Rosett.

STATEMENT OF MS. CLAUDIA ROSETT, JOURNALIST-IN-RESIDENCE, FOUNDATION FOR DEFENSE OF DEMOCRACIES

Ms. ROSETT. Thank you. Chairman Poe, Chairman Salmon, and Ros-Lehtinen, thank you for the chance to testify here today.

The administration tells us that the JCPoA cuts off all Iran's pathways to the bomb. That is simply not true. It does not cut off the pathways to North Korea. And I would be glad to provide you details on the shipping routes.

For more than three decades, as you have just heard, they have been partners in arms, and North Korea's chief role in that partnership has been as a munitions back shop for Iran's Islamic Republic. At this point, as you know, North Korea has conducted three nuclear tests, is making nuclear warheads, estimated even by China to be reaching into the double digits, helped Iran's client state Syria build a reactor that was under construction for years before it was discovered and destroyed in 2007 by an Israeli air strike. It beggars belief that Syria dared do that without Iran playing some part in it. And they are—oh. One more item. Our top military officials have been testifying and saying to the press that they assess that North Korea has the capacity to fit a nuclear warhead on an ICBM, meaning they can target us, and if the Iranians get that, guess what they can target too?

The two countries are diplomatic allies as well. This is based not just on weapons but on a shared hostility to the United States. They are both regimes—this is vital to understand—based on the coercive perfection of mankind, and they have expressed this. The current Supreme Leader of Iran, Ali Khamenei, went to visit the founding tyrant of North Korea in 1989, and they both celebrated in Pyongyang together their shared hostility to the U.S. I can give you much more recent examples. One of the first meetings that Iranian's nuclear negotiator, Javad Zarif, had in Iran after the first round of nuclear talks in Vienna last year was with a North Korean envoy.

This deal in particular gives North Korea—gives, I am sorry, Iran—a gift to North Korea as well—four things that will make it more attractive for these two countries to collaborate specifically on nuclear development. One is the snapback sanctions, which actually are a disincentive for the United States and its partners to call out Iran for cheating. The penalty is basically to blow up the deal, and this means Iran will have to go very far before anyone calls it out. Perversely, that makes it safer for North Korea to cheat, specifically on nuclear matters with Iran.

Second, money, obviously lots of money. In fact, the rounding terms in the money that Iran will get dwarf North Korea's annual merchandise trade exports.

The third is procurement access. Iran will have far freer access globally both to the financial system and to markets, much easier to buy illegitimate goods. North Korea and Iran partner in weapons development. As convenient, you will have a procurement channel through Iran's overseas illicit networks. While inspectors are watching Iran, you are going to have to watch the rest of the globe. Much harder to detect.

Finally, nuclear research and development, which will be given to Iran, yes, for civilian purposes, but even things as basic as welding, advanced welding skills, can be of great use to North Korea in its weapon programs to be fed back to Iran. And this research and development is to include workshops and training from America and its partners in thwarting sabotage of nuclear facilities.

The administration is entirely secretive about anything to do with Iranian-North Korean nuclear cooperation. Many accounts in the press. What is missing is confirmation from the administration. That Congressional Research Service report notes that Congress might wish to ask the administration for much more classified information to be declassified. The flow of that has greatly dwindled in recent years.

Finally, the point I would really like to stress is that these deals for North Korea have been not regime transforming, but regime sustaining. That is the lesson that Iran has certainly read into the failed North Korea deals that we have done, from which North Korea emerged with a nuclear bomb.

The answer would not be to conclude another nuclear deal with North Korea. It is time that Washington focused on a real strategy and plan for bringing down the regime in Pyongyang. There is no other answer to their nuclear weapons, and it would be the most salutary message that could possibly be sent to Iran because the message would be that nuclear weapons do not make it easier for tyrannies to survive.

Thank you very much.

[The prepared statement of Ms. Rosett follows:]

Congressional Testimony

The Iran-North Korea Strategic Alliance

Claudia Rosett
Journalist-in-Residence
Foundation for Defense of Democracies

Joint House Foreign Relations Subcommittee Hearing
Subcommittee on Asia and the Pacific; Subcommittee on
Terrorism, Nonproliferation and Trade; Subcommittee on
the Middle East and North Africa

Washington, DC
July 28, 2015

FOUNDATION FOR
DEFENSE OF DEMOCRACIES  1726 M Street NW • Suite 700 • Washington, DC 20036

Claudia Rosett   7/28/2015

Chairman Poe, Ranking Member Keating, distinguished members of the
committee, thank you for the invitation to testify at this hearing on the Iran-
North Korea Strategic Alliance, and how it will likely be affected by the nuclear
deal with Iran.

This is a question with serious implications for the security of America and our
allies, not only in the Middle East, but in Asia, and around the globe. I wish the
answer were reassuring.

The Administration tells us that the Joint Comprehensive Plan of Action cuts off
all Iran's pathways to the nuclear bomb. That is not true. This deal will not cut off
the pathways between Iran and nuclear-proliferating North Korea.

Worse. the JCPOA creates conditions and incentives that are highly likely to
result in the expansion of what is already an extensive and profoundly dangerous
Iran-North Korea partnership in proliferation.

In the context of the Iran-North Korea alliance, I am listing here four of the most
egregious features of the JCPOA. There are many provisions of this deal that are
profoundly troubling in any context, but I have focused on those most likely to be
exploited by Iran and North Korea working in partnership. I shall then provide
further background on the nature of the Iran-North Korea alliance, and why, on
this front, the JCPOA is likely to contribute not to peace, but to proliferation.

**1) The "snapback" sanctions mechanism, which will actually make it
safer for Iran to cheat.** In theory, this provision will keep Iran in check. But
the snapback is structured in such a way that it provides disincentives for the
U.S., or its partners, to confront Iran in the event Iran does cheat (which it has a
long record of doing, and has done even during the recent nuclear talks). The
JCPOA expressly forbids individual countries to unilaterally impose or reimpose
nuclear-related sanctions. If Iran is caught cheating, the penalty must come via
the United Nations Security Council, where it would be binary -- either nothing,
or the official reimposition of all previous U.N. sanctions. In practice, that could
take years to implement, if possible at all. But under the JCPOA, Iran could
immediately scrap its commitments, pocket its gains, and walk away. The JCPOA
itself notes that "if sanctions are reinstated in whole or in part, Iran will treat that
as grounds to cease performing its commitments under this JCPOA in whole or in
part."[1]

The disincentive to finger Iran for cheating is already evident in the most recent
report from the UN Panel of Experts on Iran sanctions, released this June. The
U.N. panel noted that during the year since its previous report, in June, 2014, not

---

[1] "Joint Comprehensive Plan of Action," Vienna, July 14, 2015, paragraph 37.
(http://www.eeas.europa.eu/statements-eeas/docs/iran_agreement/iran_joint-comprehensive-plan-of-action_en.pdf)

a single U.N. Member State had submitted a formal report of Iran's non-compliance -- despite "numerous reports in the media" that Iran's arms transfers "have actively continued." The U.N. experts noted that this lack of reporting was unusual, and speculated that while it might be linked to a decrease (they did not suggest an absence) of prohibited Iranian activities, it might also be due to "restraint" by the Member States, "so as not to affect the negotiations process."[2]

If the Member States were that conspicuously restrained during the talks, we can expect historic inertia in reporting under the deal itself.

What does that mean for North Korea, which is under international sanctions? Given the incentives the snapback mechanism creates for the world to ignore cheating by Iran, it will actually become safer for North Korea to do illicit business with Iran. Any country wishing to report or penalize North Korea for clear evidence of forbidden traffic with Iran could be left grappling with the large knock-on prospect of potentially triggering the collapse of the entire JCPOA -- and the pressure of the international community to show "restraint."

2) Money. With the lifting of sanctions, Iran obtains access to an estimated $100 billion or more upfront, in unfrozen oil revenues, plus the freedom to sell oil in the world market, without the cost of dodging sanctions. At the margin, this is likely to generate many billions more for Tehran in coming years.

That leaves Iran's regime with a lot more hard cash not only to fund terrorist proxies such as Hezbollah and Hamas, but also to go shopping in North Korea. Iran has done plenty of illicit business in Pyongyang, maintains a large embassy there, and for Iran, a major benefit of shopping for weapons and weapons technology in North Korea is that the authorities won't protest. They will be partners on the other side of the deal.

For North Korea, Iran's JCPOA jackpot may well augur boom times for the proliferation racket. While North Korea economics statistics are elusive, to say the least, political economist Nicholas Eberstadt, of the American Enterprise Institute, estimates North Korea's total merchandise trade exports for 2011 at about $4 billion, most of that to China. As Mr. Eberstadt wrote to me in a recent email: North Korea's merchandise trade "is tiny compared to the prospectively unfrozen Iran funds. No less important -- North Korea is on a permanent hunt for foreign subventions, and even a very small share of those unlocked monies would be a huge windfall for Pyongyang."

3) Procurement. Under the JCPOA, Iran obtains access to world markets and the world financial system. While the JCPOA proposes to restrict and supervise Iran's nuclear procurement, and retains the arms and missile embargoes for five

---

[2] United Nations, "Final Report of the Panel of Experts established pursuant to resolution 1929 (2010), S/2015/401*, June 2, 2015, (http://www.un.org/ga/search/view_doc.asp?symbol=S/2015/401)

and eight years, respectively, Iran will be broadly free of strictures on commerce. Much of the resulting trade may be legitimate. But the smuggler's art -- in which Iran and North Korea are both well versed -- is to hide the illicit wares amid the legitimate goods and transactions. While the snapback mechanism leaves U.N. Member States more reluctant to report violations by Iran, it will become easier for Iran to deal in forbidden goods and services abroad, and harder to detect such traffic -- including any weapons-related deals with North Korea. Such deals often run through fronts in third countries, such as China, or multiple cut-outs around the globe.

For an example of how Iran and North Korea's networks mesh, take the case of a company called Hong Kong Electronics, which was designated by the U.S. Treasury in 2009. If it sounds like a company in Hong Kong, it is not. Hong Kong Electronics was designated as a North Korean front, moving millions in proliferation-related funds, which had "facilitated the movement of money from Iran to North Korea" on behalf of another designated major North Korean proliferator, KOMID.[3] The address of Hong Kong Electronics is on Kish Island, Iran.[4]

4) Easy access to modern nuclear technology, including defense against nuclear sabotage. Under the JCPOA, developed countries are encouraged to assist Iran with civilian nuclear research. This will involve the transfer of advanced technologies and skills, which Iran, with its personnel pipelines to Pyongyang, could easily pass along to North Korea -- potentially for mutual benefit in work that would be well out of sight of any inspectors in Iran.

Not least, the JCPOA envisages "training and workshops" to strengthen Iran's security against "nuclear security threats, including sabotage." This is to be provided via cooperation between the P5+1 (the U.S., U.K. France, Russia, China and Germany) "and possibly other states as appropriate." There can be little doubt that advanced modern training to thwart sabotage would be of interest not only to Iran, but to the North Korea -- which, in return, could most easily pay in its own special coin of weapons and weapons technology.

In sum, the highly likely effect of these JCPOA provisions is that while inspectors are focused on Iran's declared facilities, or haggling with Iran over access to other domestic sites, Iran will have money, access and enhanced ability to shop the world markets, with less likelihood of being called out for illicit procurement, and approved access to an array of modern nuclear training, research and development.

---

[3] Department of the Treasury, Press Release, "Treasury Targets North Korea's Missile Proliferation Network," June 30, 2009. (http://www.treasury.gov/press-center/press-releases/Pages/tg191.aspx)
[4] Department of the Treasury, Recent OFAC Actions, June 30, 2009.
(http://www.treasury.gov/resource-center/sanctions/OFAC-Enforcement/pages/20090630.aspx)

How is that likely to affect the Iran-North Korea alliance? As summed up neatly to me last week by a 37-year veteran of the Department of Defense, Robert Collins, who specializes in analyzing North Korea's political system and the behavior of its regime: "The North Koreans who couldn't walk into nuclear Walmart, now they have Iran." And Iran will have North Korea.

So, how likely is it that Iran would really dare cheat on the JCPOA with North Korea? For insight, let us turn to some highlights of the Iran-North Korea alliance.

Background: The Iran-North Korea Partnership

North Korea is a rogue state which for more than three decades has served as a prolific munitions back shop for Iran, and is now building a nuclear arsenal -- which by various estimates could soon include dozens of warheads, and which China recently warned could include as many as 40 warheads by next year.[5] Despite international condemnations and sanctions, North Korea has carried out at least three nuclear tests, in 2006, 2009 and 2013, and since early last year has been threatening a fourth nuclear test of a "new form."[6]

North Korea, a longtime supplier to Iran of missiles and missile technology, is also working on missile delivery systems for nuclear weapons. This spring, the commander of the North American Aerospace Defense Command, Admiral Bill Gortney, told reporters at a Pentagon press briefing that North Korea has the ability --- though still untested -- to fit a miniaturized warhead on a road-mobile KN-08 intercontinental ballistic missile, and shoot it at the U.S. mainland. The commander of U.S. Forces in Korea, General Curtis M. Scaparrotti, delivered the same message in testimony to the Senate Armed Services Committee.[7]

Close ties between Iran and North Korea date back to the early days of Iran's 1979 Islamic revolution, and North Korea's supply to Iran of conventional arms and knock-offs of Soviet Scud-B short-range missiles during the 1980-1988 Iran-Iraq War. Both Iran and North Korea also were participants in Pakistan's A.Q. Khan nuclear proliferation network.

Despite the obvious differences between Iran and North Korea, theirs is a natural alliance. Weapons hungry Iran has oil. Oil-and-cash-starved North Korea makes

---

[5] Jeremy Page and Jay Solomon, "China Warns North Korean Nuclear Threat is Rising," The Wall Street Journal, April 22, 2015. (http://www.wsj.com/articles/china-warns-north-korean-nuclear-threat-is-rising-1429745706)
[6] Narae Kim, Richard Borsuk, "North Korea condemns U.N., threatens a 'new form' of nuclear test," Reuters, March 30, 2014. (http://www.reuters.com/article/2014/03/30/us-korea-north-nuclear-idUSBREA2T04020140330)
[7] Richard Sisk, "US General Tells Senate North Korea Can Hit US With Nuclear ICBM," Military.com, April 16, 2015, (http://www.military.com/daily-news/2015/04/16/us-general-tells-senate-north-korea-can-hit-us-with-nuclear-icbm.html)

weapons. Typically, North Korea is the supplier and Iran the client, though as their arsenals have become more advanced, there are reports that technology has flowed both ways. They have quite likely cooperated in their nuclear weapons programs -- a topic on which both there have been many reports in the media, but current and previous Administrations have shared far too little information with the public.

In North Korea's record of nuclear proliferation, the star item is the saga of its extensive help to Iran's client state, Syria, in building a clandestine nuclear reactor -- which the Central Intelligence Agency has dubbed the Al-Kibar reactor -- on the Euphrates River, in Syria's eastern Deir Ezzor province.This reactor, which had no visible purpose except to produce plutonium for nuclear weapons, was years in the making before it was discovered, and was nearing completion when it was destroyed in 2007 by an Israeli air strike.

Though it is widely known that North Korea helped with the design of Syria's Al-Kibar reactor, it is perhaps less well-known that North Korea also played a big part in procuring materials for the reactor. One of the chief procurement agents, a North Korean named Yun Ho-jin, was as a former North Korean ambassador to the International Atomic Energy Agency in Vienna. In 2010, The Wall Street Journal reported that Yun, along with another North Korea, Chun Byung-ho, "oversee Pyongyang's vast arms-trading network, which appears to be spreading. They have shipped components for long-range missiles, nuclear reactors and conventional arms to countries including Iran, Syria and Myanmar."[8] Currently, Yun is designated on the U.N.'s North Korea sanctions list as director of North Korea's Namchongang Trading Corporation (which is also under U.N. sanctions for proliferation activities "of grave concern") with the note: "oversees the import of items needed for the uranium enrichment programme."[9]

Concerns about further North Korean proliferation projects persist to this day, as do undocumented allegations and unanswered questions about whether Iran -- patron state of Syria and ally of North Korea -- played a role in the Syrian-North Korean Al-Kibar nuclear reactor venture.

As recently as Feb. 26, 2015, Director of National Intelligence James R. Clapper testified to the Senate Armed Services Committee that:

"North Korea's export of ballistic missiles and associated materials to several countries, including Iran and Syria, and its assistance to Syria's construction of a

---

[8] Jay Solomon, "North Korean Pair Viewed as Key to Secret Arms Trade," The Wall Street Journal, August 31, 2010.
(http://www.wsj.com/articles/SB10001424052748704741904575409940288714852)
[9] United Nations, Press Release, SC/9708, July 16, 2009.
(http://www.un.org/press/en/2009/sc9708.doc.htm)

nuclear reactor, destroyed in 2007, illustrate its willingness to proliferate dangerous technologies."[10]

While the Iran-North Korea alliance is based primarily on weapons traffic, it is fortified by a shared hostility toward free societies, as epitomized by America. Iran's Supreme Leader Ali Khamenei has underscored this aspect of Iran-North Korea relations for decades. Back in 1989, Khamenei -- then president of Iran -- traveled to Pyongyang to meet with North Korea's founding tyrant, Kim Il Sung. In a statement to Kim during that visit, Khamenei said: "Anti-Americanism can be the most important factor in our cooperation with the People's Democratic Republic of Korea."[11]

That Anti-American factor endures. In 2012, the first year of the rule of North Korea's young third-generation tyrant Kim Jong Un, two of North Korea's signal foreign policy moves were to violate a missile moratorium negotiated with the U.S. (the so-called Leap Day Deal) and then sign a scientific and technological cooperation agreement with Iran. Present at that signing, which took place with with great ceremony in Tehran, were top Iranian nuclear and military officials. Khamenei gave the North Korean delegation an audience, and celebrated the deal with a derogatory reference to the U.S., noting that Iran and North Korea "have common enemies since the arrogant powers can't bear independent governments."[12]

In testimony to the House Foreign Affairs Committee on March 5, 2013, former State Department official David Asher, an expert on North Korean illicit networks, warned that this 2012 Iran-North Korea scientific agreement bore ominous similarities to a deal that North Korea signed in 2002 with Syria, which Asher described as the "keystone" for the "covert nuclear cooperation between Iran and Syria, which ultimately resulted in the construction of a nuclear reactor complex and possibly other forms of WMD cooperation."[13]

The Question of Direct Nuclear Cooperation Between Iran and North Korea

There have been many reports in the media of direct nuclear cooperation between Iran and North Korea, including stories of Iranian officials present at

---

[10] James Clapper, "Statement for the Record: Worldwide Threat Assessment of the US Intelligence Committee, *Testimony to the Senate Armed Services Committee*, February 26 2015, (http://www.armed-services.senate.gov/imo/media/doc/Clapper_02-26-15.pdf)
[11] Associated Press, "Khamenei, in North Korea, Attacks U.S.,"May 15, 1989, (http://www.apnewsarchive.com/1989/Khamenei-in-North-Korea-Attacks-U-S-/id-8427cb998cf64b66459d48d60ceedce6)
[12] Jay Solomon, "Iran-North Korea Pact Draws Concern," The Wall Street Journal. March 8, 2013. (http://www.wsj.com/articles/SB10001424127887323628804578348640295282274)
[13] David Asher, "North Korea's Criminal Activities: Financing the Regime," *Testimony Before the House Committee on Foreign Affairs*, March 5, 2013; http://www.cnas.org/sites/default/files/publications-pdf/Asher%20Testimony%20HFAC%2003052013_0.pdf)

North Korean nuclear tests, and North Koreans visiting nuclear facilities in Iran. Many of these accounts are highly plausible, but track back to anonymous sources. They are undocumented. Just this May, an exiled Iranian opposition group, the National Council of Resistance of Iran released a report alleging that a delegation of North Korea nuclear and missile experts had visited Iranian military facilities, including a nuclear weapons research facility, this April, during the Iran nuclear negotiations.[14] The NCRI is worth paying attention to; this is the group that in 2002 exposed Iran's secret uranium enrichment facility at Natanz and heavy water facility at Arak. But once again, the sources were anonymous; the allegations undocumented.

Last July, in testimony before the House Foreign Affairs Subcommittee on Asia and the Pacific, the State Department's then-Special Representative for North Korea Policy, Glyn Davies, provided at least a glimmering of official insight on this issue. Asked by a Committee member if it was likely that North Korea would share future nuclear test data with Iran, and whether it's a concern that North Korea and Iran "have cooperated in the past," Mr. Davies replied: "I think there's every incentive between them to cooperate on some aspects of this."[15]

I would add, North Korea. for all the scrutiny it receives, is a venue where Iran might well be able to out-source a nuclear test and and hide it in plain sight -- doubling as a North Korean test.[16] North Korea is the only country in the world known to have conducted nuclear weapons tests in the 21st century (the most recent, prior to that, were India and Pakistan in 1998).

The missing element in this long-running drama is any official confirmation by the U.S. government of nuclear cooperation between Iran and North Korea. When asked about this, Administration officials tend to respond that they of course take such allegations seriously, and will look into them. There the discussion ends.

It is tempting to conclude that during the second term of the Bush administration, when North Korea conducted its first nuclear tests, officials did not want to confirm such allegations because they were hoping to cut a nuclear deal with North Korea. And under President Obama, officials have clammed up because they were hoping, as they have now done, to cut a nuclear deal with Iran.

---

[14] John Irish, "North Korean nuclear, missile experts visit Iran - dissidents," Reuters, May 28, 2015. (http://uk.reuters.com/article/2015/05/28/uk-iran-northkorea-dissidents-idUKKBN0OD08020150528)

[15] Glyn Davies, "Twenty Years of U.S. Policy on North Korea: From Agreed Framework to Strategic Patience," *Oral Testimony before the House Foreign Affairs Subcommittee on Asia and the Pacific*, July 30, 2014. (http://foreignaffairs.house.gov/hearing/subcommittee-hearing-twenty-years-us-policy-north-korea-agreed-framework-strategic-patience)

[16] Claudia Rosett, "Iran Could Outsource Its Nuclear-Weapons Program to North Korea, The Wall Street Journal, June 20, 2014. (http://www.wsj.com/articles/iran-could-outsource-its-nuclear-weapons-program-to-north-korea-1403303442)

In a report released this May, the Congressional Research Service repeated its statement of last year, that "there is no evidence that Iran and North Korea have engaged in nuclear-related trade or cooperation with each other, although ballistic missile technology cooperation between the two is significant and meaningful..."

But in the same report the CRS noted that its information focused "primarily on unclassified and declassified U.S. Intelligence Community Assessments." This suggests they could not rule out the possibility of classified evidence that might contradict their conclusion. At the end of the report, the CRS further noted that "Congress may wish to consider requiring additional reporting from the executive branch on WMD proliferation. The number of unclassified reports to Congress on WMD-related issues has decreased considerably in recent years."[17]

I would strongly urge that there be more transparency from the Administration on the question of Iran-North Korea nuclear cooperation. Or, if U.S. intelligence on this issue is so bad that Administration officials are at a loss, perhaps they could turn for help to someone within their ranks at the State Department: Assistant Secretary, Bureau of Public Affairs, Douglas Frantz.

Prior to joining the State Department, Mr. Frantz spent 35 years as a star newspaper reporter and editor, writing books on nuclear proliferators, and sharing a Pulitzer Prize for his coverage of the aftermath of Sept. 11. On August 4, 2003, Mr. Frantz published a lengthy, in-depth report in the Los Angeles Times, headlined "Iran Closes In On the Ability to Build a Nuclear Bomb." In this story, he reported that: "North Korean military scientists recently were monitored entering Iranian nuclear facilities. They are assisting in the design of a nuclear warhead, according to people inside Iran and foreign intelligence officials. So many North Koreans are working on nuclear and missile projects in Iran that a resort on the Caspian coast is set aside for their exclusive use."[18]

The State Department has refused my repeated requests to make Mr. Frantz available for an interview on this topic. It might be worthwhile for Congress to inquire of Secretary of State John Kerry what he makes of Mr. Frantz's 2003 account of lively nuclear cooperation between Iran and North Korea, and why the Administration has not confirmed any such information. Is it available only to "foreign intelligence officials"? There's every reason to believe Mr. Kerry respects Mr. Frantz's investigative and reporting skills. Before employing Mr. Frantz at the State Department, then-Senator Kerry employed him as deputy staff director and chief investigator of the Senate Foreign Relations Committee.[19]

[17] Paul K. Kerr, Steven A. Hildreth, Mary Beth D. Nikitin. "Iran-North Korea-Syria Ballistic Missile and Nuclear Cooperation," Congressional Research Service, May 11, 2015. (http://www.fas.org/sgp/crs/nuke/R43480.pdf)
[18] Douglas Frantz, "Iran Closes In on Ability to Build a Nuclear Bomb," Los Angeles Times, August 4, 2003. (http://articles.latimes.com/2003/aug/04/world/fg-nuke4)
[19] Department of State, biography of Assistant Secretary Douglas Frantz. (http://www.state.gov/r/pa/ei/biog/213904.htm)

Iran and North Korea's Nuclear Negotiations Playbook

For purposes of analyzing the Iran-North Korea alliance in the context of the JCPOA, there is at least one more angle that is vital to at least consider. With the JCPOA, the U.S. and its Western partners are effectively gambling that this deal will either greatly moderate the terror-sponsoring, despotic character of Iran's regime (with its chants of "Death to America" and threats to obliterate Israel), or at least buy time for its transformation -- preferably before the lifting of the arms embargo in five years, the missile embargo in eight, and the sunset clauses on nuclear restrictions in 10 years, 15 and beyond.

The irony is that this deal, with its gifts to Tehran, makes reform of Iran's regime less likely. This is not the first time that western negotiators desperate for a deal have dished out concessions which actually increase the dangers.

The model is North Korea, which over the past 21 years has cut a series of nuclear climbdown deals, cheated, pocketed the gains and walked away. The North Korean nuclear deals turned out to be not regime-transforming, but regime-sustaining.

Iran's regime, with its close ties to Pyongyang, and shared interest in proliferation, has surely paid close attention to how North Korea gamed the U.S.

The first of these North Korean deals was the 1994 Agreed Framework, signed under President Clinton, in which the negotiators on America's side of the table offered huge concessions, hoping -- as former IAEA expert Olli Heinonen testified last week -- "that the North Korean regime would not live a very long time."[20] At the time, North Korea was in crisis; its Soviet patron had collapsed, its founding tyrant, Kim Il Sung, died as the talks were about to begin. Defenders of the Agreed Framework like to argue that they at least delayed North Korea's nuclear progress. My counter-argument is that the Agreed Framework, with its aid, fuel, plans for two modern lightwater reactors and de facto legitimization of North Korea's second-generation tyrant Kim Jong Il, quite likely rescued the North Korean regime from a collapse that would have spared us the virulent and far more dangerous situation on the Korean peninsula today.

The Agreed Framework also allowed North Korea to retain the spent fuel rods from its Yongbyon reactor. Years later, having cheated on the nuclear deal, and -- when confronted by the Bush administration in 2002 -- walked away, North Korea retrieved the spent fuel from the Yongbyon cooling pond, and reprocessed

---

[20] Olli Heinonen, "The Iran Nuclear Deal and Its Impact on Terrorism Financing." *Oral Testimony Before the House Financial Services Committee, Task Force to Investigate Terrorism Financing*, July 22, 2015. (http://financialservices.house.gov/calendar/eventsingle.aspx?EventID=399373)

it into plutonium for its first nuclear test, in 2006. It does not take great imagination to see how this might apply on a far worse scale to Iran's retention of its nuclear infrastructure under the JCPOA.

The failure of the Agreed Framework was followed, during the Bush administration, by the 2005 Six-Party Agreement and the 2007 Denuclearization Action Plan. Both offered concessions to North Korea in exchange for promises of denuclearization. Both failed, punctuated by North Korea's first nuclear test in 2006, followed by its second and third nuclear tests, on President Obama's watch, in 2009 and 2013 -- and accompanied by the transition of power in late 2011 to North Korea's third-generation current tyrant, Kim Jong Un.

Now comes the Iran nuclear deal, replacing sanctions with vistas of cash and technology. If you believe Iran's regime sincerely plans to transform itself, and that all oil-rich Tehran ever really wanted was a large-scale civilian nuclear power program, complete with uranium enrichment facilities, for its electrical grid, then the JCPOA may seem a good bet. If, on the other hand, you think there's a chance Iran is pursuing its own variation on the North Korean playbook, that script leads to the bomb, quite possibly much sooner than even those JCPOA sunset clauses suggest.

Mr. POE. Thank you, Ms. Rosett.
Dr. Niksch, 5 minutes.

STATEMENT OF LARRY NIKSCH, PH.D., SENIOR ASSOCIATE, CENTER FOR STRATEGIC AND INTERNATIONAL STUDIES

Mr. NIKSCH. Thank you, Mr. Chairman. One thing about my resume I should mention is that the main element of my career——
Mr. POE. Is your mike on, sir?
Mr. NIKSCH [continuing]. I have been an alumnus of the Congressional Research Service for 43 years, where I worked on East Asian security issues——
Mr. CHABOT. Sir, if you could pull the mike a little closer too, it would be helpful. Thank you.
Mr. NIKSCH [continuing]. Including the Iran-North Korean issue in the late 2000s.

I want to address this policy of nondisclosure and denials coming from the executive branch about the North Korean-Iranian nuclear collaboration. And I have seen this for a number of years, going back into the Bush administration and continuing today. This has resulted in a relative obscurity of this issue in Washington. And the contrast here between these denials and this nondisclosure policy of the executive branch is the large volume of reports about both missile and nuclear collaboration between Iran and North Korea by reputable news media organs based on a large body of information provided to them by non-U.S. officials, intelligence officials, and intelligence reports in the U.K., Germany, Japan, Israel, South Korea, and Australia.

I think these sources and the volume of this material conclusively makes the case that there is not only high-level missile collaboration between North Korea and Iran, but there is also high-level nuclear collaboration between North Korea and Iran.

Now, these non-U.S. sources basically lay out, I think over the years, several stages in how this Iran-North Korean strategic relationship has developed. I want to highlight stage three, which it seems to me began about 2011. Prior to that time, most of the flow of cooperation, benefits, and assistance flowed out from North Korea to Iran, but after 2011, I have seen a reverse flow from Iran into North Korea, expanding Iranian investment of personnel and money in North Korea's domestic nuclear and missile programs. Iranian missile scientists were stationed in North Korea for a large part of 2012, well into 2013, to assist North Korea in preparing for that successful 2012 long-range missile test. And Representative Mike Rogers, then chairman of the House Intelligence Committee, was quoted in November 2013 that Iran and North Korea were working together to test engines for inter-continental ballistic missile.

Now, what is the danger of this high level of collaboration, again, in both missiles and nuclear weapons? There is, I would argue, an immediate danger, and that is in North Korea's success since at least early 2013 in developing, and I think by this time probably mounting nuclear warheads on its intermediate-range Nodong missiles.

Reports from Richard Engel of NBC News, Chris Nelson in the Nelson Report, and other statements from South Korean officials,

I think, make it clear that North Korea has made this singular achievement in its nuclear weapons program.

The danger immediately from this—and reports are that production of these warheads is increasing. That is what the Chinese nuclear experts told our people in February in Beijing. The danger simply is this: Iran's Shahab-3 intermediate-range missile is a twin of the Nodong, developed with considerable North Korean assistance. Nodong nuclear warheads will be, and I believe are, compatible with the Shahab-3. A North Korean-Iranian agreement to share Nodong nuclear warheads, it seems to me, is a realistic possibility at this stage. North Korea and Iran have had successful sea and air clandestine transportation networks. There have been few interdictions of these networks. The transfer of Nodong warheads from North Korea to Iran would have a good chance of success. And given the forecast for production increases in North Korea, you could see a real danger of this developing, it seems to me, as early as 2016. Thus, if this happens, Iran would have a secret stockpile of nuclear warheads, in Iran, that it could unveil at any time of its own choosing and thus present the United States, Israel, and the rest of the world with a fait accompli, regardless of what happens with the Iran agreement or anything else that goes on with the Iranian nuclear program.

[The prepared statement of Mr. Niksch follows:]

Larry Niksch

**Senior Associate, Center for Strategic and International Studies
Fellow, Institute for Corean-American Studies
Professor of East Asian Security Studies, George Washington University**[1]

**Testimony to the House Committee on Foreign Affairs
July 28, 2015**

The Iran-North Korea Strategic Relationship

Obscurity in Washington versus Extensive Coverage Overseas

The Iran-North Korea Strategic Relationship is an issue that has drawn minimum public attention in Washington since at least 2007 when I wrote extensively about it in a report I authored at the Congressional Research Service and updated for the next three years: *North Korea's Nuclear Weapons Development and Diplomacy* (section on Nuclear Collaboration with Iran and Syria). This, despite the extensive coverage of the major advances in the nuclear weapons and missile programs of North Korea and Iran since that time.

A major reason for this has been the reluctance—I would say unwillingness—of the Executive Branch of the U.S. Government to disclose information about the Iran-North Korea relationship. There have been some public disclosures about Iranian-North Korean collaboration in the development of missiles. On nuclear collaboration, there has been a virtual blackout of public information. As my former colleagues at the Congressional Research stated in a recent report (*Iran-North Korea-Syria Ballistic Missile and Nuclear Cooperation*), officials of the Executive Branch have stated that there is "no evidence that

---

[1] The views expressed are those of the author and do not represents views of the organizations with which the author is affiliated.

Iran and North Korea have engaged in nuclear-related trade or cooperation." This blackout includes this denial, avoiding specific answers when asked about this, and denial statements in unclassified and declassified U.S. intelligence assessments.

Thus, little has appeared in the American news media about this. There are, however, a couple of notable exceptions. In September 2012, Iran and North Korea signed an agreement for wide-ranging technology and scientific cooperation. This did draw a reaction from Obama Administration officials, which the *Wall Street Journal* reported on March 8, 2013. The report asserted that Obama Administration officials were concerned that the head of Iran's Atomic Energy Agency was present at the signing ceremony. It described U.S. officials as concerned that Iran and North Korea share nuclear technology.

The *Washington Post* reported on November 7, 2011, that "secret intelligence" provided to the International Atomic Energy Agency showed that Iran had received "crucial technology" from North Korea for the development of nuclear warheads. This included mathematical formulas and codes for warhead designs "some of which appear to have originated in North Korea."

On missile collaboration one of several notable reports came from the *New York Times* on November 28, 2010. This report cited "secret American intelligence assessments" that North Korea had supplied Iran with 19 intermediate range missiles in 2006 with a range of up to 2,000 miles. This missile today is known as the Musudan, which North Korea has displayed on several occasions. (It should be noted that several experts have expressed doubt about the accuracy of this report and the intelligence assessments cited in the report.)

Nevertheless, the public information from the Bush and Obama Administrations, the State Department, and the U.S. intelligence agencies has been sparse. A major reason seems to have been that the Bush and Obama Administrations have sought to avoid dealing with the North Korea-Iran strategic relationship in U.S. nuclear talks with North Korea. In 2007 into 2008, the Bush Administration resisted requests from the House Foreign Affairs Committee and the House Intelligence Committee for information on North Korea's involvement in the Syrian nuclear reactor, which Israel had bombed in September 2007. Only after the committees escalated pressure did the Administration brief Members on the reactor and North Korea's involvement in late April 2008. Even then, however, the Bush Administration did not reveal the rest of the story: Iran's involvement in the Syrian reactor. Revelations of Iran's involvement later came from Israeli officials, the Japanese newspaper, *Sankei Shimbun*, and the German newspaper, *Der Spiegel*. *Der* Spiegel revealed in a lengthy article of November 2, 2009, that a high-ranking Iranian defector revealed the existence of the Syrian reactor to Israeli and U.S. intelligence agencies and Iran's financing of the reactor.

Moreover, in April 2008, the Bush Administration negotiated an agreement with North Korea that removed from North Korea the obligation in the six party agreement of February 2007 that North Korea issue a "complete and correct" declaration of its nuclear programs. Consequently, the North Korean declaration of June 26, 2008, contained no information about North Korea's nuclear proliferation activities or its uranium enrichment program. In short, the Bush Administration chose to avoid dealing with North Korea over its nuclear collaboration with Iran and Syria.

With North Korea's declaration, the Bush Administration removed North Korea from the official U.S. list of state sponsors of terrorism. The Obama Administration has continued the removal. The State Department continually states that the U.S. Government has no evidence that North Korea is supporting international terrorist groups. At a meeting I attended in June 2010, a State Department official dealing with the Middle East said she was "not prepared" to comment on a question whether North Korea was a source of missiles to Hezbollah. In contrast, Secretary of Defense Robert Gates stated in San Francisco on August 12, 2010, that "North Korea continues to smuggle missiles and weapons to other countries around the world—Burma, Iran, Hezbollah, Hamas." Hezbollah and Hamas are designated by the U.S. Government as international terrorist organizations. In 2014, there were new reports that North Korea was negotiating with Hamas to provide missiles and communications equipment to Hamas.

The State Department's defacto denials of North Korean assistance to Hezbollah and Hamas is another indication of the Bush and Obama Administration's policy of avoidance of dealing in U.S. diplomacy with the issue of Iran-North Korea collaboration. Numerous reports describe the Iranian Revolutionary Guards as the main foreign supporter of Hezbollah and Hamas and the facilitator of North Korean assistance to these groups.

This pattern appears to be followed in the new Iran nuclear agreement. There is no known provision related to Iran-North Korea nuclear collaboration in it. The National Council of Resistance of Iran (NCRI) is a group of some controversy, but it has issued detailed reports in the past—some confirmed as accurate--about Iran's nuclear program and North Korea's collaboration with Iran. It reported on May 28, 2015, that a North Korean delegation of nuclear warhead and missile experts had visited Iran under tight security and had held meetings with Iranian counterparts. The National Council claimed that this was the third visit of the North Korean delegation in 2015. When asked about this, a State Department spokesman gave a previous standard answer to questions about NCRI reports that "we take such reports seriously" but "we don't have information at this time." The spokesman added that given the absence of information, the allegations would not "impact our ongoing negotiations over Iran's nuclear program."

The obscurity of this issue in Washington and the apparent policy motives behind it contrast strongly with the extensive coverage given overseas to Iran-North Korean collaboration, especially nuclear collaboration. Reputable newspapers in Great Britain, Germany, Japan, South Korea, Israel, Australia, and even Russia have contained a volume of reports since the late 1990s on the building Iran-North Korea collaboration in developing missiles and nuclear warheads. They frequently cite non-U.S. intelligence sources and reports, senior European and German defense officials, Japanese diplomatic officials and intelligence sources, Israeli government officials (including intelligence officials), South Korean intelligence sources, high-level North Korean and Iranian defectors, and sources within the Iranian regime. Other reports cite as sources "foreign intelligence officials" and "western intelligence sources." Information from German intelligence and defense officials is especially prominent in these reports. This may explain why Germany has been included with the five permanent members of the U.N. Security Council in the negotiations over the current Iran nuclear agreement.

Two major foreign news organs, the *Sydney Morning Herald* and *Reuters News* have quoted from non-U.S. intelligence reports on the Iranian-North Korean collaboration. The Australian newspaper, in 2005, quoted from a three page intelligence report describing a secret course North Korean nuclear experts were conducting in Tehran on developing nuclear technology for possible military uses. The Reuters report, in May 2010, quoted from "an intelligence report from a non-U.S. diplomat" in Vienna that North Korean nuclear experts were continuing to instruct Iranians in developing nuclear technology. Both media organs quoted IAEA officials that the intelligence reports were credible.

It seems to me that the volume of non-U.S. reports and the sources cited give the information in them credibility in spite of the dearth of similar U.S. information. This further supports my conclusion that there are distinct policy reasons of the Bush and Obama Administrations behind the obscurity of the Iran-North Korea collaboration issue in Washington.

The Evolution of Missile and Nuclear Collaboration

The many reports about Iran-North Korea collaboration together portray an evolving relationship with collaboration becoming more intense and varied. It seems to me that there have been three stages in collaboration since the 1990s. The first is that between the seller of arms—North Korea—and the buyer—Iran. This has involved Scud and Nodong missiles, component parts of missiles, and conventional arms including arms ultimately bound for Hezbollah and Hamas.

There also may have been a transfer of nuclear materials from North Korea to Iran. In March 2010, Leonard Spector, deputy director of the Monterey Institute of International Studies' James Martin Center for Non-Proliferation Studies, said in a column in the Center's website that North Korea had shipped 45 tons of unenriched uranium concentrate, ie., "yellowcake," to Syria, which was moved to Iran.

By the late 1990s, the relationship evolved into more permanent institutional collaboration. This appeared to begin when North Korea sent missile experts to Iran to help Iran develop indigenous production facilities for the Shahab-3 intermediate range missile. The Shahab-3 is a twin of North Korea's Nodong missile. The original Shahab-3s contained complete Nodong components transferred from North Korea. The North Koreans then established working ties with Iranian companies responsible for producing missiles. The most important of these appears to be with the Iranian Shahid Memmat Industrial Group (SHIG). SHIG is part of the network of the Iranian Revolutionary Guards. North Korean missiles experts reportedly have worked in the SHIG facilities in

Iran, including work on upgrading the Shahab-3 and other Shahab class missiles. SHIG delegations reportedly frequently visit North Korea, including visits to observe North Korean missile tests.

The nuclear technology courses taught by North Koreans in Tehran cited above is another example of this institutional collaboration. Another group of North Korean instructors reportedly went to Tehran in February 2011 to teach Iranian Revolutionary Guard and Iranian Defense Ministry officials how to operate a specialized computer program that simulates neutron flows. According to the German newspaper, *Suddeutsche Zeitung*, "western secret services sources" described this program as "vital" for the development of nuclear warheads.

A body of non-U.S. reports have emerged since the early 2000s pointing to an institutional collaborative Iran-North Korea relationship inside Iran. North Korea's principle interlocutor has been the Iranian Revolutionary Guards but also some joint work with the Iranian Defense Ministry and Atomic Energy Agency. From 2003 on, there have been a volume of reports that North Korean nuclear and missile experts have been stationed in Iran working with these Iranian organizations on research and development of missiles and nuclear warheads. (See my CRS Report, North Korea's Nuclear Weapons Developments and Diplomacy, for descriptions of these reports from 2003 to 2010).

In 2011, a special committee under the U.N. Security Council, set up to monitor implementation of U.N. sanctions against North Korea, issued a report. The report was not made public, reportedly because of opposition from China. However, major portions of the report leaked to media organs. It seems to me that the report presented an accurate summary of the state of Iran-North Korea collaboration at that time. It asserted that North Korea and Iran were suspected of exchanging missile technology, using a third country" as a conduit (undoubtedly China). It described exchanges of scientists and technicians, exchange of data, reciprocal participation in nuclear and missile tests, and joint work analyzing the results of tests.

This institutional collaboration apparently is continuing, according to numerous reports since 2011 asserting that there have been several hundred North Korean nuclear and missile experts in Iran. One of latest reports came in *The Christian Science Monitor* (February 20, 2015), which cited South Korean intelligence sources that there were "hundreds" of North Korean nuclear and missile experts in Iran.

It seems to me that one of the questions about the Iran nuclear agreement is whether it will result in an identifiable exodus of these North Koreans from Iran, or whether the status of these people will remain largely unknown. Will North Korean nuclear and missile delegations continue to visit Iran, or will this be stopped? That being said, it also seems to me that the third stage in Iran-North Korean collaboration has the biggest connection to the Iran nuclear agreement.

This third stage appears to have begun about 2011. It may be connected to the technology sharing agreement Iran and North Korea signed in September 2012. The Ayatollah Khamenei attended the signing ceremony and declared that Iran and North Korea have "common enemies" and had established an "anti-hegemonic front." But it may be even more connected with the report of Japan's Kyodo News (July 23, 2012) that Iran and North Korea signed a secret agreement in April 2012 to deepen collaboration on bilateral "strategic projects." According to Kyodo correspondent, Tomotaro Inoue (currently a Kyodo correspondent in Washington), his source, a "diplomatic insider" told him that a senior Iranian nuclear official, Saeed Jalili, lobbied Iranian President Mahmoud Ahmadinejad, to send officials to North Korea to conclude such an agreement.

As the September agreement and reportedly the April agreement were signed, reports have emerged that Iran has sent missile experts and possibly nuclear experts to North Korea to be stationed there permanently or semi-permanently. Kyodo, United Press International, the Korea Herald (Seoul) and Reuters News all reported that Iranian missile experts arrived in North Korea in the early fall of 2012 to help the North Koreans prepare for the test launch of a long-range missile in December 2012. That test was successful. The UPI report identified the Iranians as officials of Shahid Hemmat Industrial Group (SHIG). The South Korean newspaper, *Chosun Ilbo*, cited a South Korean government source describing cars traveling from the likely living quarters of the Iranians to the test site for the December 2012 launch. Subsequent reports assert that SHIG officials continually visited North Korea throughout 2013 for extended stays. An additional report from a publication, Open Source Intelligence, authored by former Deputy Assistant

Secretary of the Army Van Hipp, asserted that Iran had stationed in North Korea up to 100 nuclear scientists and technicians.

Representative Mike Rogers, Chairman of the House Intelligence Committee, was quoted in November 2013 that Iran and North Korea were together testing engines for an intercontinental ballistic missile. (Washington Free Beacon, November 27, 2013) The North Korean Government has boasted openly that this program is intended to develop an intercontinental ballistic missile that could hit U.S. territory with a nuclear warhead.

We also have the report, again from Kyodo, that an especially high level Iranian delegation traveled to North Korea to observe the February 2013 nuclear test and that Iranian President Ahmadinejad approved the payment of "tens of millions of U.S. dollars" to North Korea in order to observe the test. The Kyodo report identified a Chinese bank, Bank of Kunlun in Beijing, as the bank through which the payment to North Korea was made. The London *Sunday Times* cited "western intelligence sources" that Iran's leading nuclear scientist, Mohsen Fakhrizadeh-Mahabadi, was believed to have traveled to North Korea to observe the nuclear test. According to U.S., European, and Israeli press reports, Mohsen has been described as the key scientist in Iran's program to develop a uranium warhead for Iranian missiles based on North Korean technology. He is said to be a target for assassination by Israel.

At the time of the nuclear test, the U.S. publication, *Investor's Business Daily* quoted a "senior American official" who seemed to give partial credibility to these reports. He said that "it's very possible that the North Koreans are testing for two countries (ie., Iran)."

This third stage has at least two implications. One is that Iran now is investing heavily in North Korea's domestic missile and nuclear programs both in terms of committing personnel in North Korea to participate in these programs and probably also in terms of financial investment (more about Iranian money later). The previous largely one way relationship of North Korean experts working in Iran has become a more mutual relationship. This raises the crucial question of what Iran expects to gain from its commitment to North Korea's programs. The second implication is that, if the reported Iranian investment in observing North Korea's February 2013 nuclear test is correct, that test likely was the test of a uranium warhead designed to fit on to a missile. Iran would not have made that kind of investment just to observe a third plutonium test; the Iranians, according to numerous reports, had observed the two earlier plutonium tests.

The Potential Dangers

The immediate potential danger in the wake of the Iran nuclear agreement lies in North Korea's major nuclear weapons achievement to date: the development of a nuclear warhead that can be fitted on the Nodong intermediate range missile. North Korea's National Defense Commission, chaired by Kim Jong-un, issued a statement on May 20, 2015, claiming major advances in developing missiles and nuclear warheads for missiles. All U.S. attention, including much skepticism, focused on North Korea's claim that it had perfected a long-range missile and a nuclear warhead for that missile. That skepticism appears accurate, at least for now. However, the National Defense Commission also alluded to "nuclear striking means" on "medium and short-range rockets." That claim, it seems to me, is credible.

On April 3, 2013, Richard Engel, the long-standing national security correspondent of NBC News, reported that U.S. officials told him that they believe North Korea had developed nuclear warheads for missiles with a range of 1,000 miles. That North Korean missile is the Nodong. Chris Nelson reported in the Nelson Report (read by the author and most Korea-watchers) of May 5, 2013, that within the U.S. Government, the likelihood that North Korea had developed nuclear warheads for the Nodongs "seems far more certain behind closed doors than in public." On July 28, 2014, Wi Sung-lac, South Korea's Ambassador to Russia, was quoted by the *Korea Herald* that "Since North Korea can mount nuclear warheads on its rockets, our task is to counter these real threats." Subsequently, the Commander of U.S. Forces in Korea, General Curtis Scaparrotti, said he believed that North Korea has "the capability to miniaturize a [nuclear] device" and the "technology to potentially deliver what they say they have." Many non-government North Korea experts also believe that North Korea is producing nuclear warheads for the Nodongs.

China also appears to have reached this conclusion. In February 2015, a team of Chinese nuclear experts met with American counterparts in Beijing. One of China's top uranium enrichment experts told the Americans that the U.S. estimate of North Korea's nuclear weapons stockpile (10-16 weapons) was too low. He stated that North Korea probably had 20 warheads at the end of 2014 and enough weapons-grade uranium to double that number within one year. Such an output would be in the form of nuclear warheads for missiles, probably first for the Nodong. The Nodong can reach targets throughout South Korea and most of Japan. I would add that the Chinese estimate is similar to recent estimates put out by Joel Wit of the Johns Hopkins School of Advanced International Studies and David Albright of the Institute of Science and International Security.

I have detailed these reports because the Obama Administration has not publicly disclosed that North Korea has succeeded in developing nuclear warheads for the Nodong missile—and by this time no doubt mounting warheads on several of the missiles. The Defense Intelligence Agency stated in an assessment made public in April 2013 (the time of the Richard Engel report) that it had "moderate confidence the North currently has nuclear weapons capable of delivery by ballistic missiles." Immediately, officials of both the White House and the Pentagon issued counter statements that they had seen no evidence that North Korea had such capabilities.

The South Korean Government of President Park Geun-hye also has tried to downplay the Nodong warhead story but with less success. Besides Ambassador Wi's statement cited above, South Korea's Defense Minister stated in November 2013 that "we evaluate that North Korea can build a nuclear weapon using uranium." An R.O.K. Defense Ministry White Paper released on January 6, 2015, stated that North Korea had "considerable" technical capability to mount warheads on missiles.

The Obama Administration and Park Administration have their reasons for not wanting to disclose that North Korea has developed nuclear warheads for the Nodongs. For the Obama Administration, an admission would undermine the long-standing U.S. position that the United States will "never recognize" North Korea as a nuclear weapons state. Admission would be politically harmful to the President since North Korea's achievement came "on his watch." Thirdly, the Administration likely fears that disclosure of Nodong warheads would raise questions about Iran's involvement in the program at the time the Administration has been negotiating the Iran nuclear agreement minus the issue of Iran-North Korea nuclear collaboration.

There also is the possibility that the Administration would seek to keep the Nodong warhead issue off the negotiating table if it resumed nuclear negotiations with North Korea. In meetings I have attended, previous Obama Administration officials have stated that in future negotiations with North Korea, the Administration should focus on achieving a freeze on nuclear and missile testing in order to prevent North Korea from advancing toward its stated goal of developing an ICBM and nuclear warhead that could reach the United States. Such a negotiating strategy likely would see the United States seeking to put the Nodong warhead issue on the sidelines.

It seems to me that the Obama Administration's non-disclosure policy increases the already present danger that Iran's growing investment in North Korea's nuclear and missile programs has an objective of acquiring Nodong nuclear warheads. Knowing that the Obama Administration and possibly the next U.S. administration would resist disclosing North Korea's development of Nodong warheads, Iran and North Korea undoubtedly would be more emboldened to seal such an arrangement and start transferring nuclear warheads to Iran as North Korea's production increases. Moreover, under a non-disclosure policy, if a U.S. intelligence agency discovered that North Korea was shipping nuclear warheads to Iran, the Obama Administration or a successor Administration might be less inclined to inform the IAEA and/or the U.N. Security Council.

Iran's Shahab-3 missile is a twin of the Nodong, developed with considerable North Korean input. According to estimates by the U.S. Air Force and the Institute of International Security Studies in London, Iran reportedly has at least 50 Shahab-3 missiles. A nuclear warhead that would fit the Nodong would fit the Shahab-3. The Shahab-3 could reach Israel and other targets in the Middle East.

If China's estimate is accurate, North Korea's output of Nodong warheads may be sufficient by 2016 for Iran to acquire a number of these warheads. They could be shipped by sea or transported by air from North Korea to Iran. Shipments would use Chinese ports (where weapons cargos are transferred to different ships multiple times) and airports as transfer and concealment points as North Korea has done relatively successfully for missile and weapons shipments to Iran and Syria. For example, U.S. intelligence officials were quoted in April 2015 in the *Washington Free* Beacon (April

15, 2015) that North Korea had transported successfully at least two shipments of missile components to Iran since September 2014.

China likely would do little to prevent this. It has done nothing substantive in the past to prevent North Korea and Iran from using Chinese ports, airports, and banks as conduits for their collaboration. China views the Iran nuclear agreement as opening the way to proceed with plans to build economic and energy relations with Iran, which China had to postpone when U.N. sanctions were imposed on Iran a few years ago. China can be expected to proceed with its aims of bringing Iran fully into its Asian Infrastructure Bank (Iran is a member) and promoting Iran's membership in Xi Jin-pings's proposed Asian continental security organization.

Once in Iran, continued concealment likely would succeed until the warheads reached hidden storage sites or hidden Shahab-3 missile sites. (Since the early 2000s, reports have described North Korean assistance to Iran in constructing underground facilities to conceal weapons.) Iran then would have a secret nuclear weapons capability that it could unveil instantly at a time of its choosing. The so-called one year break out time that the Iran nuclear agreement is supposed to impose on Iran would be neutralized. If Iran decided to reactivate its nuclear weapons program, Shahab-3s with nuclear warheads would give it an immediate nuclear deterrence against any military action that the United States or Israel might contemplate.

During my work on this issue at the Congressional Research Service, one of my prime sources of information was Takashi Arimoto, correspondent of the Japanese newspaper, *Sankei Shimbun*. Mr. Arimoto provided me with information about North Korea's activities in the Middle East that almost always turned out to be accurate. In the 1990s, he wrote the first expose that North Korea had been supplying arms to the Tamil Tigers in Sri Lanka. When he returned to Japan, he continued to follow the North Korea-Iran relationship and send me information that he had obtained from his sources.

Sankei Shimbun published an article by Mr. Arimoto on February 9, 2011, citing Japanese sources knowledgeable about North Korea. It was close to a "blockbuster." Mr. Arimoto asserted that North Korea and Iran had entered into a secret agreement during the 2008-2010 period under which North Korea would ship a certain portion of its produced enriched uranium to Iran. Such an arrangement would be activated if Iran's own uranium enrichment facilities became unusable. Given the nature of Iranian-North Korean collaboration, Mr. Arimoto's report hardly seems illogical. If true, the question now becomes: Would this sharing arrangement be enlarged to include Nodong nuclear warheads if the Iran nuclear agreement shuts down or limits Iran's own warhead program?

Iran's contribution to North Korea's successful test of a long-range missile in December 2012 appears to signal that Iran is interested in the longer term to benefit if North Korea succeeds in developing a missile and nuclear warhead that could hit the United States. There appears to be little in the Iran nuclear agreement that would prevent Iran from continuing or increasing its personnel and financial investments in North Korea's future missile and nuclear warhead programs.

Iranian Money: Lubricant for the Wheels of Iran-North Korean Collaboration

The reports of the different facets of Iranian-North Korean collaboration sometimes contain estimates from the non-U.S. intelligence and government sources that Iran has paid North Korea huge sums of money for cooperative projects related to missiles, nuclear warheads, and Pyongyang's assistance to Hezbollah and Hamas. As stated previously, the Kyodo report on Iranians observing the 2013 North Korean nuclear test referred to Iran paying tens of millions of U.S dollars to North Korea. The *Suddeutsche Zeitung* report of North Korea providing a nuclear computer program to Iran cited the newspaper's sources as saying that Iran may have paid up to $100 million for the program. In 2009, the Institute of Foreign Policy Analysis issued a report estimating that North Korea earned about $1.5 billion annually from its missile collaboration with Iran alone.

It seems to me that North Korea may receive from Iran upwards of $2 to $3 billion annually from Iran for the various forms of collaboration between them. Mr. Arimoto's report on the secret Iran-North Korean agreement on enriched uranium sharing stated that Iran paid North Korea $2 billion during the 2008-2010 period to finance Pyongyang's uranium enrichment program. There should be no doubt that North Korea drives a hard financial bargain with Iran for the benefits it provides to Iran. As the collaboration has deepened and North Korea has expanded its programs, North Korea's asking price no doubt has risen. One estimate is that the cost of North Korea's long range missile test of December 2012 was $1.3 billion. Iran at this stage may be financing the bulk of the costs of North Korea's nuclear and missile programs.

Iranian money appears to be the lubricant for North Korea's nuclear and missile programs. The Iran nuclear agreement will increase Iran's wealth considerably as U.N. economic sanctions are lifted and Iran receives at least $50 billion from the United States in frozen assets. If Iran pursues its escalated investment in North Korea's nuclear and missile programs, more Iranian money likely will flow to North Korea. It always is possible that North Korean leaders will get overly-greedy and will repel the Iranians. But Iran's greed for benefits from North Korea's nuclear, missile, and terrorist-supporting assistance also appears to be growing, so the match likely will continue despite the Iran nuclear agreement.

———

Mr. POE. I thank the gentleman. Members of Congress will ask you questions, so you can continue your statement.

Dr. Walsh.

STATEMENT OF JIM WALSH, PH.D., RESEARCH ASSOCIATE, SECURITY STUDIES PROGRAM, MASSACHUSETTS INSTITUTE OF TECHNOLOGY

Mr. WALSH. Mr. and Madam Chairs and Ranking Members, it is an honor to be with you today. In my remarks, I will focus on the single most important question regarding any Iran-North Korea relationship: Will Iran look to North Korea to help cheat on the nuclear deal?

First, we need to ask, how should policymakers assess the risk of Iran-North Korea cheating? As I told the Senate Foreign Relations Committee, assessment is more than simply listing things that could go wrong. In theory, lots of things can happen, but in practice, very few of those possibilities come true. Experience and data enable analysts to distinguish between what is likely and what is unlikely.

I would like to review with you the evidence available on this critical question. One piece of evidence, Iran's past nuclear behavior. The DNI has repeatedly testified that Iran had a structured nuclear weapons program that begin in the late 1990s and was halted in 2003. These activities represent a clear violation of Iran's NPT obligations and provide a cause of concern that Iran might violate its commitments in the future.

A second source of evidence, Iran's current capabilities and intentions. The DNI reported in 2012 that ''Iran has the capacity to eventually produce nuclear weapons, making the central issue its political will to do so''—not technical, political. ''. . .We assess Iran is keeping open the option to develop nuclear weapons should it choose to do so. We do not know, however, if Iran will eventually decide to build nuclear weapons.''

To state it plainly, Iran does not currently have an active nuclear weapons program. It has no active covert weapons facilities, nuclear weapons facilities, and has not made a decision to pursue nuclear weapons. Of course, Iran could change course in the future, and the U.S. should take steps to minimize that possibility and be prepared to respond. Nevertheless, as a matter of risk assessment, these are favorable conditions for a nuclear agreement.

On its face, it would seem odd for Iran to, A, have no weapons program; B, not to have made a weapons decision; C, agree to the most intrusive verification regime ever negotiated in a multilateral nonproliferation agreement; and D, then decide to cheat.

Three, Iran-North Korea nuclear relations. Missile cooperation between Iran and North Korea has been well documented. Nuclear cooperation between the two is a different matter, however. People who believe there has been nuclear cooperation rely almost exclusively on media accounts. I have reviewed some 76 media reports covering a span of 11 years. None of the 76 reports has been confirmed—none. On the other side of the ledger, the DNI, the IAEA, the U.N. Panel of Experts for Iran, and the U.N. Panel of Experts for North Korea, despite numerous opportunities to do so, have never claimed Iranian-North Korean nuclear coordination. The

Congressional Research Service concluded, ''There is no evidence that Iran and North Korea have engaged in nuclear-related trade and cooperation.''

It is worth pointing out that Iran and North Korea chose completely different paths for their weapons efforts. North Korea pursued a plutonium route, while Iran focussed on enrichment. At one point, North Korea decided to develop enrichment, but the centrifuges it fielded appeared to be different and more advanced designs than Iran's. So if Iran is helping North Korea, why are Iran's centrifuges worse?

Finally, let me address the effects of the nuclear agreement on these risks. I judge that the agreement reduces the incentives for nuclear cooperation. First, if we find evidence of that cooperation, no matter how small, it will constitute a prima facie violation of the agreement. Second, it would require cross-regional transfers of people and material, which increases the risk of detection. Already we have ample cases of countries interdicting shipments by North Korea. Third, Iran would have to worry about the prospect that a North Korean defector might spill the beans. Iran will be sensitive to this possibility insofar as it is an alleged Russian that outed Iran's nuclear program in the early 2000s.

Fourth, the mercurial nature of North Korea's young Kim Jong-un, complete with leadership purges and questionable behavior, might rightly give Iran pause at choosing it as a partner.

Fifth, as a result of the agreement, surveillance on North Korea will likely increase, if only because governments fear such cooperation. And it will not simply be the U.S. that is doing the watching. Saudi Arabia and others will be motivated actors. Increased surveillance makes any cooperation between the two daunting and risky.

In conclusion, I assess it is unlikely that Iran would attempt to cheat by collaborating with North Korea. Moreover, if it did, the chance that they would be detected would be substantial.

Thank you.

[The prepared statement of Mr. Walsh follows:]

Dr. Jim Walsh
Research Associate, MIT Security Studies Program

House Committee on Foreign Affairs
Committee on Foreign Affairs
U.S. House of Representatives
        Subcommittee on Terrorism, Nonproliferation, and Trade
        Subcommittee on Asia and the Pacific
        Subcommittee on the Middle East and North Africa

"The Iran-North Korea Strategic Alliance""

Tuesday, July 28, 2015

Committee on Foreign Affairs
U.S. House of Representatives
Subcommittee on Terrorism, Nonproliferation, and Trade
Subcommittee on Asia and the Pacific
Subcommittee on the Middle East and North Africa

"The Iran-North Korea Strategic Alliance"
"

Tuesday, July 28, 2015

Statement of Dr. Jim Walsh
MIT Security Studies Program

Mr. Chairmen, Mr. Ranking Members, and Members of the Committee:

It is an honor to be with you today to discuss Iran, North Korea, and the recently concluded Joint Comprehensive Plan of Action (JCPOA).[1]

As a matter of background, I come to this topic with a life-long emphasis on international security, and in particular of proliferation and nuclear weapons decision-making. I have always worked on a bipartisan basis, providing assessments to Republican and Democratic Administrations, as well as to Republican and Democratic Members of Congress, as they have worked with proliferation challenges. As regards Iran and the Democratic People's Republic of Korea (DPRK), I have studied and written about their nuclear programs for more than 15 years. I have been to both Iran and North Korea and have spent hundreds of hours in meetings with Iranian and DPRK officials respectively discussing nuclear and related issues.

1. The Central Question and Summary Judgment

---

[1] I would like to thank the many people who helped with my testimony, including Angela Nichols, Greg Thielmann, Daniel Wertz, Tim MacDonald, Stephen Van Evera, Taylor Fravel, Michelle Lee, and Vipin Narang, to name a few.

In my testimony, I will focus on what I consider to be the single most important of question concerning the Iran-DPRK relationship: <u>Will North Korea help Iran cheat on the nuclear deal?</u>

My summary judgment, explained in detail below and based on the available evidence in the public domain, is that <u>it is unlikely that Iran will use the DPRK to cheat on this agreement</u>.

2. How should policymakers assess the risk of Iran-DPRK cheating?
Assessment is more than simply listing the things that could go wrong (or right) with an agreement. In theory, lots of things can happen, but in practice few of those possibilities come true. Experience and data enable analysts to distinguish between what is more likely and what is less likely. This, in turn, makes it possible for policymakers to weigh costs, benefits, and tradeoffs.

In addition, one should be clear about the standard for judging risk. The question is not whether a given agreement is risk free. In all public policy making there is risk: risk from action and risk from inaction. Zero risk is simply not possible. Still, it may be possible to distinguish risk among competing alternatives.

As regards Iran, the DPRK, and the risk of cheating, analysts and policymakers can draw on multiple sources of data to help estimate risks. These include:

  1) Past Iranian behavior
  2) Iran's current capabilities and intentions
  3) Iranian-DPRK relations (past and present)
  4) Evidence from nuclear history
  5) New incentives and disincentives introduced by the JCPOA

3. Past Iranian behavior
Iran's previous behavior is a logical place to begin, and the record suggests that cheating should be a concern. The Director of National Intelligence (DNI) has repeatedly testified that Iran had a structured nuclear weapons program that began in the late 1990s and that was halted in 2003, a conclusion echoed by other country's assessments and implied in various IAEA reports on Iran. These activities represented a clear violation of Iran's Nuclear Nonproliferation Treaty (NPT) obligations and provide cause for concern that Iran might violate its

commitments in the future. These illicit activities included the surreptitious construction of enrichment facilities and centrifuges.

Since the public disclosure of its enrichment program, Iran has allowed International Atomic Energy Agency (IAEA) inspection of its enrichment facilities, though it did not grant the Agency full and enduring access to all sites of interest (e.g., the heavy water production facility and the Arak reactor construction site).

The IAEA also reports that Iran has complied with the Joint Plan of Action (JPOA), which has been in effect for a little more than a year and a half.

Based on Iran's past violations during the period of the late 1990's to 2003 and efforts to cover up those violations, I conclude that --absent other conditions-- there is a nontrivial risk Iran might attempt to circumvent its obligations, that is, cheat.

4. Iran's current capabilities and intentions

The most authoritative guides to Iran's nuclear program are the IAEA reports and the DNI's testimony and statements. In 2012, the DNI reported that:

> "Iran has the ...capacity to eventually produce nuclear weapons, making the central issue its political will to do so. ...We assess Iran is keeping open the option to develop nuclear weapons, ... should it choose to do so. We do not know, however, if Iran will eventually decide to build nuclear weapons."[2]

He went on to say that Iran's nuclear choices reflect a cost-benefit approach.

These conclusions, which have been publicly affirmed at levels of high confidence for 9 years in a row, have direct implications for risk assessment. To state it plainly, Iran does not have an active nuclear weapons program, has no covert weapons-related facilities, and has not made a decision to pursue nuclear weapons.

---

[2] James R. Clapper, "Unclassified Statement for the Record on the Worldwide Threat Assessment of the U.S. Intelligence Community for the Senate Select Committee on Intelligence," Office of the Director of National Intelligence, January 31, 2012, p 6, http://www.intelligence.senate.gov/120131/clapper.pdf.

This state of affairs would, in turn, suggests that if Iran were to turn to the DPRK for help with a nuclear weapons program, it would require two decisions Iran has not made, i.e. it would require a reversal of its current policies. Iran would have to:

1) Decide to acquire nuclear weapons, which it has not done, and

2) Decide to conspire with DPRK to achieve that end

Of course, Iran could change course in the future if conditions or Iran's leadership changes, and as a matter of policy-making, the United States and the international community should take steps to minimize that risk and be prepared to respond should Iran choose to change course. Nevertheless, as a matter of risk assessment, these are favorable conditions for a nuclear agreement.

On its face, it would seem odd for Iran to a) have no weapons program, b) have not made a weapons decision, c) agree to the most intrusive verification regime ever negotiated in a multi-lateral nonproliferation agreement and *then* d) decide to cheat.

5. Iranian-DPRK nuclear relations (past and present)

Just as Iran's past behavior, in this case it's violations of its NPT commitments, should help inform an assessment of Iran's potential future actions, Iran's past and present relations with the DPRK should be considered as they relate to possible collaboration between the two countries.

North Korea's support for the Islamic Republic dates back to the 1980s and the Iran-Iraq War, when Pyongyang provided arms and other support to Tehran. Missile cooperation between the two has been well documented, and Iran has confirmed as much, though there continues to be debate over whether that trade in missile continues today and the relative status of each country's missile program. (These questions are discussed in detail in Appendix I.)

The critical questions, however, are 1) whether there has been bi-lateral cooperation in the nuclear field, and in particular as it relates to nuclear weapons, 2) if there was nuclear cooperation in the past, might it reoccur in the future, and 3) if there was not nuclear cooperation, would past (or present) ties in the missile field become the basis for future nuclear weapons cooperation.

The general logic behind possible nuclear cooperation is the same as it is for missile cooperation. First, there is the principle of "my enemy's enemy is my friend" – or at least my opportunistic trading partner. Bolstering that basic logic is the fact that both countries have faced sanctions on their missile and nuclear programs and thus would seem to have an incentive to collaborate insofar as alternative sources of support are largely unavailable.

As regards joint nuclear weapons work, there have been a number of media reports suggesting such cooperation as well as allegations made by the MEK and its affiliated groups.[3]

I have reviewed some 76 media reports covering a span of 11 years (2005-2015).[4] More than half of these reports (42) occur in the last 2 years, with 30 taking place in 2015 alone. About a third of those are from media that most observers would associate with a particular ideological point of view (e.g., the Free Beacon, the Tower, and Anti-War.com). It would appear that the dramatic increase in these reports in 2014 and 2015 reflects the fact that the Iran negotiations were progressing to a final agreement rather than objective changes on the ground. Again, in this regard it is worth remembering the DNI finding that Iran halted its nuclear weapons program in 2003. In any case, none of the 76 reports has been confirmed. In addition, assertions by the MEK, like virtually every allegation made by the MEK following its first accurate claim regarding Iran's enrichment facilities, have also failed to find confirmation.

On the other side of the ledger:

> **The DNI despite numerous opportunities to do so, has never claimed Iranian-DPRK nuclear coordination even as the DNI has pointed to missile cooperation between the two countries and testified as to Syrian-DPRK nuclear cooperation.

> **The IAEA has never alleged nuclear cooperation between Iran and North Korea.

---

[3] On the MEK, a group that until recently was on the US government's list of terrorist groups, see Ronen Cohen, *The Rise and Fall of the Mojahedin Khalq 1987-1997*, Sussex Academy Press, Brighton: 2009.

[4] I am indebted to Tim MacDonnell and Michelle Lee for their research on this topic.

**The UN Panel of Experts for Iran Sanctions and the UN Panel of Experts for North Korea Sanctions have never claimed joint IRI-DPRK nuclear activities.[5]

**A 2015 Congressional Research Service review of the data leads it to conclude that," there is no evidence that Iran and North Korea have engaged in nuclear-related trade or cooperation with each other..."[6]

**Virtually no journal article in the scholarly literature has claimed evidence of nuclear collaboration between Pyongyang and Tehran. The exception is Christina Lin's article in the *Middle East Review of International Affairs* (March 2010), which relies on unsubstantiated newspaper and media accounts.[7]

It is worth pointing out that the Islamic Republic and the DPRK chose completely different paths for their weapons efforts. North Korea pursued a plutonium route, while Iran focused on uranium enrichment. At one point relatively late in its weapons effort, Pyongyang decided to also develop a uranium enrichment capability, but the centrifuges it fielded appear to be a different, more advanced design than the IR-1s (Pakistani P-1s) deployed by Iran.[8]

As for the DPRK, its past nuclear behavior has demonstrated a willingness to transfer reactor technology (e.g., Syria), though perhaps not the necessary reprocessing technology.[9] More importantly for this discussion, there is no

---

[5] Not all UN Panel of Experts reports have been made public, but discussions with members of both panels substantiate the point.

[6] Paul Kerr et al, "Iran-North Korea-Syria Ballistic Missile and Nuclear Cooperation," Congressional Research Service, May 11, 2015.

[7] Christina Lin, "China, Iran, and North Korea: A Triangular Strategic Alliance," *Middle East Review of International Affairs*, Vol. 14, No. 1, (March 2010). For more skeptical and nuanced views see: Mark Fitzpatrick, "Iran and North Korea: The Proliferation Nexus," *Survival*, Vol. 48, No. 1 (Spring 2006); Jeffrey Lewis, "Limited Partnership," *Foreign Policy*, February 22, 2013. http://foreignpolicy.com/2013/02/22/limited-partnership/?wp_login_redirect=0; and Dan Wertz, "Iran-North Korea Relations: Missile and Possible Nuclear Cooperation," Working paper, July, 2015.

[8] David Albright and Christina Walrond, "North Korea's Estimated Stocks of Plutonium and Weapon-Grade Uranium," Institute for Science and International Security, August 16, 2012, http://isis-online.org/uploads/isis-reports/documents/dprk_fissile_material_production_16Aug2012.pdf.

[9] Background Briefing with Senior U.S. Officials on Syria's Covert Nuclear Reactor and North Korea's Involvement," April 24, 2008. http://fas.org/irp/news/2008/04/odni042408.pdf

evidence to date that North Korea has transferred fissile material or an actual weapon to a third party.

6. Evidence from nuclear history

Iran and North Korea are not the first countries in the nuclear age to have engaged in missile trade while harboring nuclear weapons ambitions. In the 70 years of the nuclear age, many nuclear weapons states and nuclear aspirants have engaged in missile trade with other countries that had nuclear ambitions. Yet one has not observed over time a situation in which missile trade caused the countries involved to develop nuclear trade.

In addition, those 7 decades of experience has yielded two lessons.

The first is that media reports on proliferation are unreliable. Iran and the DPRK are only the latest countries whose activities have been subject to media speculation. As someone who has studied the nuclear histories and behavior of at least a dozen countries, one regularly sees media reporting which archival evidence has subsequently proven to be false.

Second, scientific cooperation agreements, even those that have an explicit nuclear component, are poor predictors of nuclear weapons cooperation. While in many cases where nuclear cooperation does take takes place, there *is* a scientific cooperation agreement, in the vast majority of cases, a scientific cooperation agreement is not associated with nuclear weapons cooperation. In other words, such agreements can be a minimum condition but it is a poor predictor.

It also has to be said that today's nonproliferation landscape is a far more hostile environment for that kind of cooperation than in earlier decades of the nuclear era. The IAEA operates under a much stronger set of rules (e.g., the Additional Protocol) and has an array of science and technologies for verification that inspectors in the past could only dream of. There are multiple policy instruments available to the international community, like the PSI, that simply did not exist before. That does not mean that Iran-North Korea cheating cannot happen, that it is impossible. It does suggest for the purposes of risk assessment, however, that it is unlikely.

7. New incentives and disincentives introduced by the JCPOA

So far, this assessment has focused on relevant data from the past and present. But it is also worth asking what new effects of the JCPOA might have on Iran's calculus.

On the one hand, it appears that the JCPOA would increase Iran's incentive to initiate nuclear weapons cooperation with North Korea. (Again, the worst-case assumption for purely analytical purposes is that at some point in the future, Iran abandons its current policy and decides to pursue nuclear weapons.)

The JCPOA effectively blocks Iran's path to indigenously developing a bomb. If it attempted to use its declared facilities, it would be caught virtually immediately. That leaves two options: sneak out, or nuclear weapons collaboration outside its territory. This is not the place to discuss the sneak out scenario, but to the extent that the JCPOA also makes that more difficult – as it surely does given the procurement channel and the "cradle to grave" monitoring of its entire fuel cycle— it could increase the incentive to seek assistance from third parties.

On the other hand, the prospect of a joint IRI-DPRK weapons effort would not appear to be very promising, given other risks and disincentives.

7.1 If the P5+1 (or any country for that matter) finds evidence of that collaboration, no matter how small, it will constitute a prima facie violation of the agreement and Iran will be found in noncompliance.

7.2 It would require cross-region transfers of people and material, which increases the risk of detection. Already we have ample cases of countries interdicting shipments by the DPRK. The Proliferation Security Initiative's (PSI) core purpose is to prevent these kinds of transfers. It is one thing for China and North Korea to engage in illicit cross-border trade, quite another for Iran and North Korea to do it over thousands of miles fraught with multiple choke points.

7.3 Iran would have to worry about the prospect that a North Korean defector might spill the beans. Iran would be especially sensitive to this possibility, insofar as it is alleged that a Russian who worked on Iran's nuclear program was one of the sources regarding Iran's weapons program.

7.4 The mercurial nature of North Korea's young Kim Jong Un, complete with leadership purges and questionable behavior might rightly give Iran pause. Put another way, you feel comfortable entering into a high-stakes, long-term deal with Kim Jong Un?

7.5 Iran will also have to worry about the survival of the North Korean regime. Will it even be here years from now? To be sure, many analysts have lost by betting on the DPRK's demise, and it has to be said that at least economically, Pyongyang appears to be doing better in recent years, but the regime could be one famine or crisis with South Korea away from crashing. If that were to happen, Iran could be exposed.

7.6 Tehran would be risking its currently good relations with the far more wealthy and powerful South Korea, if the cooperation were discovered.[10]

7.7 As a result of the JCPOA, surveillance of North Korea will likely increase, if only because governments might fear such cooperation. And it will not simply be the US that is doing the watching. Israel, Saudi Arabia, and others that previously might not have had a direct stake in North Korean activities will be motivated actors. It is also worth noting that the UN Panel of Experts on North Korean Sanctions is not going away. It is here to stay regardless of what happens with Iran. Its work, combined with PSI, the national technical means of many different countries, and other instrumentalities would make any cooperation between the two daunting and risky.

8. Concluding Thoughts

Quality assessment requires measuring and weighing different risks. When it comes to the possibility of future IRI-DPRK nuclear weapons cooperation, the risks run both ways but the conclusions are clear.

On one side of the ledger is Iran's past cheating (during the late 1990s until 2003) and the effect of the JCPOA closing alternative routes to the bomb, which suggests that there is a risk that Iran could turn to North Korea for help.

On the other side of the ledger is the fact that Iran does not have a weapons program, has not made a decision to pursue nuclear weapons, the absence of any serious evidence of past nuclear cooperation with the DPRK, the fact that the DPRK has no record of transferring fissile material or nuclear weapons to third

---

[10] On Iranian relations with South Korea, see Azad, Shirzad, "Iran and the Two Koreas: A Peculiar Pattern of Foreign Policy," *The Journal of East Asian Affairs*, Vol. 26, No. 2, Fall/Winter 2012.

parties, the experience of the last 70 years of the nuclear age, and the enormous risks Iran would be running if it engaged in such behavior.

In weighing these risks, based on the available evidence, I assess that the chances of such cooperation are very low, that it is unlikely that Iran would attempt to cheat by collaborating with North Korea. Moreover, if they did, the chance that they would be detected would be substantial.

If one then steps back and compares the potential benefits of an agreement that blocks Iran's path to the bomb against the potential costs of IRI-DPRK cheating and other risks, it is clear that this is a very good agreement that will enhance US and global security for years to come.

It has been a great honor to appear before this august body. If I can be of service in the future, I stand ready to do so.

Thank you.

Mr. POE. I thank the witnesses.

And I recognize myself for 5 minutes for questions.

Does North Korea have nuclear weapons? That is a yes or no question.

Mr. WALSH. To whom, Mr. Chair?

Mr. POE. To all four of you. Just go down the row.

Ms. ROSETT. Yes.

Mr. POE. Go down the row.

Ms. ROSETT. Absolutely.

Mr. NIKSCH. Yes, including nuclear warheads for the Nodong missile.

Mr. POE. Okay.

Mr. WALSH. I would—they have nuclear devices. They have tested nuclear devices.

Mr. POE. Do they have nuclear weapons?

Mr. WALSH. A nuclear device is not a usable military nuclear weapon.

Mr. POE. So, no.

Mr. WALSH. It is unclear. They have tested. That has been a——

Ms. ROSETT. The head of U.S. Forces Command Korea testified to Congress this spring that they have the ability to fit a warhead on an intercontinental ballistic missile. I think that we are looking at warheads here.

Mr. NIKSCH. Richard Engel, the very experienced longstanding correspondent for NBC News, reported on April 3——

Mr. SHERMAN. Microphone.

Mr. NIKSCH [continuing]. In 2013 that his sources and contacts in the U.S. Government—and he has extensive sources——

Mr. POE. So, that is yes?

Mr. NIKSCH [continuing]. In the U.S. Government, were telling him that North Korea had succeeded in developing a nuclear warhead for a missile with a range of 1,000 miles. Now, that missile in the North Korean arsenal is the Nodong. Chris Nelson reported a month later in the Nelson Report——

Mr. POE. Thank you, Doctor. I think I got your answer was a yes.

I am reclaiming my time. I am going to ask the questions because I am going to limit myself as well as everybody else to the time. Thank you.

I know that the President of North Korea made the comment, I guess it was last year, that he was trying to develop an intercontinental ballistic missile and send it to Austin, Texas. I am offended by that to some extent, being from Texas, that he picked Austin, but the—set aside the nuclear agreement with Iran, just set that aside. Can North Korea and Iran still cooperate in mischief, like promoting terrorism, weapon development, conventional weapons? Set that whole thing aside and assume Iran will follow it as it is written.

Mr. Berman, I will ask you that question.

Mr. BERMAN. The answer is yes, sir, with caveats, which is that some of these programs are expensive. They are extensive, and they are expensive. This is why, in my opening statement, I focused on the sanctions relief that is coming in the direction of Iran in the near term. Because this cooperation is ongoing now when

Iran is under sanctions and the North Koreans are hurting for cold hard cash.

You heard Dr. Niksch talk about the ''reverse flow.'' Part of that has to do with the fact that, as Iran becomes reintegrated into the global economic community, it will have greater money to spend on collaboration with other countries, including North Korea.

Mr. POE. Okay. Let me reclaim my time, Mr. Berman. In other words, they can still work together, and Iran can still follow the deal, but they can work together. That still would have a detrimental effect to the world. For example, in the work, I will ask you, Ms. Rosett, of terrorism. Iran being the world's number one state sponsor of terror—I think North Korea should be on the list, but they are not—can Iran continue to develop its terrorist activities in the world working with North Korea to achieve that goal and still follow the deal?

Ms. ROSETT. Yes. North Korea has been of substantial assistance to Hezbollah, which is something, again, the administration has been silent on, but a Federal case in which I testified as an expert witness last year found that they have——

Mr. POE. And be specific. Where is Hezbollah doing its mischief?

Ms. ROSETT. Southern Lebanon, which is pointing right at Israel, that is. And may I also give you an illustration of how North Korea, in fact, helped with proliferation in Vienna, right where the nuclear talks were taking place, there is an enormous North Korean Embassy on the edge of town, along with a big Iranian Embassy in the middle of it. And with the Syrian reactor, it was a former North Korean Ambassador to the IAEA in Vienna who set up an enormous procurement network spanning Europe, China, Asia, which helped buy the components for the Syrian reactor that the Israelis finally destroyed in 2007. There is no reason that could not be duplicated today. He worked through China, which through these entire negotiations has still not rolled up the illicit procurement network of another Chinese proliferator to Iran, Li Fangwei, for whom there is a $5-million reward offered by the State Department, who remains active, although the U.S., since 2004, has been demarching the Chinese to please try to shut him down. So is it possible? Oh, yes, with bells.

Mr. POE. Thank you.

I will yield 5 minutes to the gentleman from Massachusetts, Mr. Keating, the ranking member.

Mr. KEATING. Thank you, Mr. Chairman.

A couple of questions for Dr. Walsh, one in terms of nuclear cooperation; the other in terms of missile cooperation.

The first one, my understanding is that Iranian and North Korean nuclear programs differ significantly in the types of fissile material and the types of centrifuges that are being used. Given those differences, how much would Iran benefit from nuclear cooperation with North Korea should that occur?

Mr. WALSH. Well, I think, Congressman, that the DNI has made it clear that Iran as a basic nuclear weapons capability, because they know how to build a centrifuge. You can't bomb that knowledge out of their head. That is why the DNI says this is not a technical issue but a political issue and why I think the agreement is a good idea, because it puts Iran on a different path. Iran hasn't decided to go for nuclear weapons, despite the media claims. The DNI says it has not made the bomb decision. This is why I think this is important.

But they were very different programs. Again, the North Koreans focused on the plutonium route. The Iranians focused on the uranium route. They don't really need the North Koreans. I mean, they are already there. The question is how do we keep them from making the decision, not how do we keep them from being there. That horse is out of the barn.

Mr. KEATING. And just to follow up on the second part, with missile cooperation, there is a lot of expert knowledge that assesses Iran has likely exceeded North Korea's ability to develop, test, and build ballistic missiles. So, in your view, would Iran have to gain— what would they have to gain from missile cooperation with North Korea? You know, how would the conclusion of the nuclear agreement with Iran affect Iran's incentive to work with North Korea in this kind of technology if so many experts believe they have already exceeded that?

Mr. WALSH. Yeah. Well, I think Iran's program has been sort of slow and steady wins the raise, and North Korea's has sort of tried to leap to the end. Iran has solid fuel rockets. North Korea doesn't have solid fuel rockets. When you have a liquid fuel rocket, that makes that rocket vulnerable to preemption and attack. So the Iranians don't want liquid fuel propulsion technology. That is not going to help them at all.

Now, to be fair, both face a problem with accuracy of their missiles and their guidance systems, but neither is in a position to help the other with that because they both have the same problem.

Mr. KEATING. Another quick question. How would you compare the two agreements, North Korea and Iranian? What was lacking in—what were some of the problems with the North Korean agreement, and have they been addressed?

Mr. WALSH. Well, you know, as a summary statement about the comprehensive agreement, any agreement that is hated by Iranian hardliners and supported by Israeli intel and military people can't be all bad, but to answer specifically your question, the Agreed Framework was 3-pages long 20 years ago. The comprehensive agreement is 159 pages in the golden era of verification. As I alluded to, it is—compared to all the other nonproliferation agreements—this is not our first rodeo. We have been doing this for 70 years. Compared to all the others, this is the strongest multinational nonproliferation agreement ever negotiated. It has unprecedented features. A dedicated procurement channel does not exist in any of the past agreements; snapback sanctions, does not exist in any of the previous agreements; the science and the mandates available to IAEA today, the additional protocol did not exist in 1994, which gives the agency the right to go to any site, military or otherwise, on Iranian soil.

And in terms of technology, we are in the digital age of verification. There were no satellites and open-source material and digital seals and environmental sampling. All of this is available to us today. This is not your father's IAEA, and this is not your father's verification system. We enjoy, as the Snowden revelations would seem to imply, robust national technical means that we can apply in addition to IAEA inspection.

Mr. KEATING. And what do you think in terms of international sanctions on North Korea? What has been their effect?

Mr. WALSH. Well, the bottom line there. It is not about Iran. Is it about China and Russia, right? We are blessed as a country in that we are surrounded by two big oceans and two big friendly neighbors. The second luckiest country in international relations, North Korea, because they are right smack next to the biggest growing economy on the planet. And as long as that is true, everything else sort of pales in comparison to that. I must add, though, that the Russians who also share a border, have been a heavy contributor in this regard.

Mr. KEATING. I yield back, Mr. Chairman.

Mr. POE. I thank the gentleman. The Chair recognizes the gentleman from Arizona Mr. Salmon.

Mr. SALMON. Thank you, Mr. Chairman.

Some say that North Korea may be less likely to selling nuclear weapons or weapon qualities of fissile material than nuclear technology or less sensitive equipment to other countries in part because it needs its limited fissile material for its own deterrent. Some believe that is possible. I am not sure that that is something I believe, but I want to throw that out there.

However, that the North might find a nuclear weapons or fissile material transfer more feasible if its stockpile is large enough or it faces an extreme economic crisis with a potentially huge revenue from such a sale could help the country survive. So my question is, what is the current estimate of North Korea's stockpile and how satisfied are they with what they have? Anybody have any ideas on that?

Ms. Rosett.

Ms. ROSETT. China gave that estimate that by next year they could have 40 nuclear warheads. They had enough for that. We also know from sources, such as David Albright's think tank here in Washington, ISIS, not the terrorist group, that the size that can be seen of the uranium enrichment plant at the Yongbyon Nuclear Complex has at least doubled since they unveiled it in 2010. Remember that they denied even having that for years. Finally, then, displayed it to an American nuclear physicist. Now it has been expanding. U.S. officials suspect there are additional hidden facilities. So it is quite substantial. And if I may also just address the different plutonium and uranium tracks. The reason that North Korea began with plutonium is the Soviets built them a reactor which they then disregarded the NPT on, and they had spent fuel which the Agreed Framework let them keep. Meanwhile, in the 1990s, they were also hosting A.Q. Khan of Pakistan's A.Q. Khan network, of which Iran was a member as well. So they actually pursued both tracks from the beginning. And this is just what you have seen Iran doing. You can argue that the Arak heavy-water reactor is now going to be filled up with cement, but you have seen the two countries, actually as quickly as they could each in their own way, pursuing these. And from China's estimates, from estimates we have had in past years, from the signs of activity, you have to consider that North Korea probably has a substantial quantity and you need to ask the following question: What for? How many nuclear warheads could North Korea use before it was hit? So anything extra you are seeing is for what? Bragging rights? For sale? One more thing, danger of bragging rights. This isn't about protecting your country. This is about sustaining your regime for both Iran and North Korea. That is what these weapons are for. And that is why they are going to go after them. It is not—Iran, if this is all about a commercial and nuclear program for Iran, this has been the most elaborate windup in human history to a civilian power project. Okay. And no, what they want are the weapons. North Korea has been going after them. I would look at China's estimates with some suspicion. It is China. But when China is saying to American nuclear scientists they can have 40 warheads by next year, you should be concerned.

Mr. SALMON. Well, I don't even think the administration is advocating that this is for peaceful nuclear purposes. I mean, this is a country that is probably more awash in oil and gas than any other. I mean, I think anybody that is naive enough to believe that they were actually creating this nuclear program for peaceful purposes deserves the award of the month or the award of the year.

Ms. ROSETT. If I may, in the JCPoA Iran reaffirms that it never will—it said it never will seek a nuclear weapon. In other words, it lies in the JCPoA. So if you are concerned about cheating, it should concern you from the beginning that it includes clear lies by the Iranian regime from the get-go. That is—also just one other thing, on the procurement networks, North Korea has road mobile KN–08 intercontinental ballistic missiles. That is what our military has been warning about. They think that these things are actually usable. Where did North Korea get the vehicles? They were sold by China. The Hubei Sanjiang space vehicle company, and when they were caught, because North Korea paraded them in 2012, China said, "Oops, we thought they were for use in logging. We sent them thinking they were being used as lumber trucks." I submit to you, beware of the similar things going on with Iran, and on the procurement channel, it operates under complete confidentiality.

If you liked Oil-for-Food, you will love the U.N. procurement, the P5+1 procurement channel for Iran's nuclear program. I am not even sure Congress will be able to see what is being approved through that. Thank you.

Mr. SALMON. Thank you. I see I have run out of time.

Mr. POE. I recognize the gentleman from California.

Mr. SHERMAN. I just want to note a few things for the record.

This new deal with Iran is more intrusive than prior deals. Those prior deals have prevented Holland from having nuclear weapon. Costa Rica doesn't have the bomb. But as far as stopping Iraq and Syria. That was bombing that stopped them from having the bomb. Qadhafi thought he was going to be destroyed; turned out he was right. South Africa, it was Mandela, and the newly independent states gave up their weapons back to Russia because the Russian Army wouldn't have it any other way.

So it is hard to say that any of the deals we have had have prevented a determined state from getting a nuclear weapon. But Costa Rica remains nuclear free. And just because the deal is more intrusive than prior deals doesn't mean it is anywhere close to being good enough. The IRGC says they are against the deal. If Iran was trying to get Congress to go along with the deal, they would put out the word that the IRGC was against the deal. So we don't know if that is genuine or for our consumption. We do know that everyone in the Israeli Government is against this. The vast majority of former officials in the Israeli Government are against this. You know, even, we have dissenting opinions in this country from the 95 percent view, but only 1 percent of the United States Senate is socialist or at least availably so. You get a range of views in any democratic country. As I think the chairman pointed out, or wrote, it is insane to think that Iran has this nuclear program as an efficient way of generating electricity. They are spending billions of dollars on it. They have incurred hundreds of billions of dollars, at least tens of billions of dollars, of sanctions to their economy, all so they could generate electricity? This is a country that flares its natural gas. So it is free natural gas. They have no other use for it. Easiest thing in the world to do is produce a natural gas electric generation facility.

Iran has the means and the motive. The means here is they are going to get their hands on $100 billion. That puts them in, some say $56 billion. I think it is considerably more than that. That puts them in a position to buy a weapon from either Pakistan or North Korea. And they certainly have the motive. Look what happens to leaders that get themselves on the American people fear-and-hate-you list, the axis of evil list. Qadhafi is dead. Saddam Hussein is dead. Kim Jong-un is alive and well and doing unusual things in North Korea because he has nuclear weapons. The Supreme Leader has not failed to notice this.

So the question is, how do we—it is beyond these hearings to talk about how to prevent Pakistan from selling nuclear weapons. There are two ways to prevent Iran from buying a nuclear weapon from North Korea. First, don't let it have its hands on $56 billion to $100 billion. Nobody is going to sell a nuclear weapon for pocket change.

The second would be controls on North Korea. And the question is, should we be prepared to keep North Korea off the terrorist list, although they deserve to be on it, and even recognize them as a nuclear weapon state providing they agree to controls—to observation, not that would prevent them from doing whatever they are going to do, just enough to prevent them from selling it to somebody else.

Mr. Berman.

Mr. BERMAN. Well, sir, let me, if I may, could I pick up on a point that you made earlier, when you were talking about the IRGC and sort of, you know, where they come down on——

Mr. SHERMAN. No, because I have got 1 minute. Go ahead.

Mr. BERMAN. Oh, okay.

Mr. SHERMAN. Stick to my question.

Mr. BERMAN. Well, in that case, I think it bears noting that what you are looking at in both countries is sort of a target of opportunity.

With regard to Iranian hardliners, they understand——

Mr. SHERMAN. I am asking about North Korea. As long as they have nuclear weapons, they might sell them. Could be Iran, could be somebody else that emerges later. Should we cut a deal with North Korea that will prevent them from surreptitious sales of a nuclear weapon and should we be prepared to give to North Korea recognition as a nuclear weapon state, agreement not to put them on the terrorist list or anything else you care to identify——

Mr. BERMAN. I don't think so, sir, for the simple reason that even if the most rosy predictions that you heard this morning at this table are true, they have not been proven out over time. And the idea that you move directly from a JCPoA with Iran to a JCPoA with North Korea stretches——

Mr. SHERMAN. Okay, anybody have a contrary view?

Mr. WALSH. Yes.

Mr. SHERMAN. Ms. Rosett.

Ms. ROSETT. Yes. May I just say, it would not work. That regime, the nuclear program in North Korea is so entrenched, so deep, so vital, they will not—you will not talk them out of it.

Mr. SHERMAN. I am not asking to talk them out I am talking about just letting us watch to make sure they don't sell.

Ms. ROSETT. They won't let you.

Mr. SHERMAN. They won't let you do that for anything we could deliver. Anybody else disagree?

Ms. ROSETT. There is a price at which they would make that deal. There is always a price. But the price would be such that they would emerge from it with yet more nuclear weapons. You would buy far worse trouble. They will not make a deal that will let you——

Mr. SHERMAN. That will prevent—okay.

Mr. NIKSCH. We haven't tried it with North Korea.

Mr. SHERMAN. And we haven't even offered them a non-aggression pact.

Mr. NIKSCH. The Bush administration basically took what was then called the proliferation issue off the table in 2008. So when North Korea had to issue a disclosure statement about its nuclear programs, North Korea did not have to say a word and did not say a word about its nuclear activities even in Syria.

Mr. SHERMAN. Let me just get in one more comment, and that is, unless it is clear that we hold China——

Mr. NIKSCH. So what you are talking about is not——

Mr. SHERMAN. Unless we hold China responsible for what North Korea does, given the fact that the existence of the North Korean regime is dependent entirely on China, or substantially on China, we are going to have to worry an awful lot about what North Korea might do in this situation or some other situation. It is China's fault that Kim Jong-un is still there.

I yield back.

Mr. POE. Okay. The Chair recognizes the gentleman from Texas, Mr. Weber, for 5 minutes.

Mr. WEBER. Thank you. I forget which one it was that said there has been reporting on the North Korea success Richard Engel and Chris Nelson. Was that you, Dr.——

Mr. NIKSCH. Richard Engel of NBC News and Chris Nelson, who writes the Daily Nelson Report, that all of us Korean watchers read daily.

Mr. WEBER. So you mentioned a date for Richard Engel of April 3, 2013, but you didn't——

Mr. NIKSCH. A report on NBC News.

Mr. WEBER. Okay, but you didn't mention a date on Chris Nelson. You say he writes daily.

Mr. NIKSCH. It was May 2, 2013.

Mr. WEBER. Okay, and you said that the—now, you also said, I think, and I don't want to put words in your mouth, that this administration—and it is probably not just this one—but has a policy of nondisclosure and denials.

Mr. NIKSCH. This goes back into the Bush administration. Both the Bush and Obama administrations have had this policy, both with regard to Iranian—North Korean nuclear collaboration——

Mr. WEBER. Got you.

Mr. NIKSCH [continuing]. And also denials that North Korea has been assisting through Iran in supporting Hezbollah and Hamas.

Mr. WEBER. Okay. Were you the one that said the Chinese told us in February that productions of warheads were increasing, and they would have about 40? Or was that——

Ms. ROSETT. That was me. And may I also just say, there is a reporter who won a Pulitzer Prize, wrote for the LA Times for many years, who wrote on August 4, 2003, that according to his sources inside Iran, and with "foreign intelligence agencies," there was evidence—he put this quite clearly—I can give you—send of the article—that North Koreas were in Iran developing—working on warheads, nuclear warheads with the Iranians. The name of that journalist is Douglas Frantz. He was the deputy chief of staff for the Senate Foreign Relations Committee.

Mr. WEBER. Frantz?

Ms. ROSETT. Frantz, F-r-a-n-t-z. It is in my written statement. He was the deputy chief of staff to John Kerry when John Kerry was a Senator, and he now works in the State Department in the Bureau of Public Affairs.

Mr. WEBER. Okay, so——

Ms. ROSETT. I have tried to interview him about that story and have been told he is not available. I would suggest that the Secretary speak with his own long-time trusted former reporter who wrote this as a documented fact in 2003.

Mr. WEBER. Okay, great. Great point. You also said, if I think, if I heard correctly, that there was a former North Korean Ambassador to the IAEA that set up the procurement channel?

Ms. ROSETT. Yes, Yun Ho-jin. He is on the U.S. designated list. He worked in Vienna. In fact, at one point he showed IAEA inspectors around the North Korea Yongbyon reactor. When the Al-Kibar reactor was discovered in Syria, he turned out to be a major procurement agent. He had been buying goods. In other words, North Korea was a very full service shop for that operation. They didn't just give them the designs. They helped them buy things worldwide. He had fronts in Europe, in Damascus, in China, and in Beijing. To this day, the administration is so secretive about this; they must know things about those transactions. They don't even give the addresses of his companies.

Mr. WEBER. What was the name of the site in Syria?

Ms. ROSETT. Sure. It was in Syria's Deir ez-Zor province. It was near a place called Al-Kibar and the CIA briefing on that, the Bush administration was also terribly secretive.

Mr. WEBER. Okay, who discovered that?

Ms. ROSETT. The Israelis discovered it.

Mr. WEBER. The Israelis discovered it.

Ms. ROSETT. They told the United States, and——

Mr. WEBER. Should we fear they have moved to Iran now?

Ms. ROSETT. I hope they are there looking. The problem is, are we listening, and does the public learn?

Mr. WEBER. Okay.

Ms. ROSETT. I mean, let me just say one more thing on that Syrian reactor. It was discovered while the U.S. was concluding a nuclear agreement with North Korea, and we were being told——

Mr. WEBER. You mean they were cheating while we were negotiating?

Ms. ROSETT. Exactly, very likely with Iranian knowledge of the whole scene. Okay, the administration should tell us more about what we want to know.

Mr. WEBER. Let me move on. I just wanted the history.

Ms. ROSETT. While we were being told the reactor was being shut down in North Korea, the North Koreans were actively building near completion the reactor.

Mr. WEBER. Got you. I appreciate that. People lie. There is a shock.

So, Dr. Walsh, you mentioned solid fuel versus liquid fuel rockets and you mentioned that snapback sanctions did not exist back in— and this wasn't your—I don't know how you said it—your father's agreement or something of that nature.

Mr. WALSH. Yes.

Mr. WEBER. And so snapback sanctions you believe now do exist, and so, in your opinion, in 24 days, if somebody goes in there and gets these sanctions back in place—and I think Secretary Kerry said that they were within 2 months of possible breakout when they started negotiating 2 years ago. So is 24 days of the supposed having a discussion over a clandestine site—that is almost a month. So if they were close to 2 months, do you, in your opinion, do you think snapback sanctions happen fast enough to prevent a 2-month breakout? Really?

Mr. WALSH. I appreciate the question because under the Joint Comprehensive Agreement, breakout times goes from a couple of months, which is today, or it was, you know——

Mr. WEBER. And you don't think they are cheating while we are negotiating?

Mr. WALSH [continuing]. Sir, to a year. Because we are removing 98 percent of their enriched material and cutting their centrifuges by two-thirds. That is what the agreement does. It extends breakout from a couple of months to a year. On those 24 days, people— there seems to be confusion about that. If IAEA wants to get into a site, Iran blocks them, and then we see trucks pulling up and ferreting stuff away, or they bulldoze the building, that is prima facie noncompliance with the agreement. Then the thing kicks in, but we have a year breakout period.

Mr. WEBER. You don't leave any room for underground tunneling of any sort where they are actually doing things underground?

Mr. WALSH. Well, we have environmental sampling. We have tunnel monitors. We have——

Mr. WEBER. After they break out in 2 months, it is a little late to be worried about——

Mr. WALSH. It is a year breakout, sir. It is a year breakout under the comprehensive agreement.

Mr. WEBER. Yeah, but they already said they were within 2 months the last time.

Mr. WALSH. No, prior to the interim agreement, prior to the JPOA——

Mr. WEBER. I get that. If you trust that everything they have they reveal to us and that we can——

Mr. WALSH. Well, the DNI says that. I am willing to go with the DNI.

Mr. WEBER. Mr. Chairman, I yield back.

Mr. POE. The Chair recognizes the gentleman from Pennsylvania, Mr. Perry.

Mr. PERRY. Thank you, Mr. Chairman.

Ms. Rosett, did I say it correctly?

Ms. ROSETT. That is correct, yes.

Mr. PERRY. Thank you. We know that both Iran and North Korea do use technology from and through China. I am wondering how China's involvement affects the relationship between Iran and North Korea, and not only in a material way but if you can, or if anybody can, the subtleties through the U.N. in anything that happens.

Ms. ROSETT. The U.N. is not your friend in this. Remember, it was—let's start with the fact that at United Nations, Iran for the past 3 years has chaired the second largest voting block in the General Assembly, the Non-Aligned Movement. The U.N.—the reason I mention Oil-for-Food is that there is considerable disincentive for any one state to call out cheating, to do anything else. It is a collective problem. And that is exactly what happened with the incredible corruption through Iraq contracts overseen by the U.N. This deal sets up a similar mechanism in which things will go through the U.N., and it is very hard to get information.

With respect to China, there is much debate about this. It is my view, and I have been covering these areas since the 1980s when I worked in Far East. I will just add, I made a trip to North Korea in 1991. I didn't need to go to Iran. There were Iranians on my plane in from Beijing to Pyongyang. They are very busy there. I have seen it.

But China, I believe, benefits from the instability that is created by North Korea. And if you ask yourself the simple question, "who do North Korea or Iran, for that matter, have an incentive to attack, and who do they have an incentive not to," I would argue that they don't chant, "Death to Russia," "Death to China." They chant, "Death to America," "Death to Israel." They are, by character of the regime, opposed to free societies. That is not frivolous. And they also don't dare attack Russia or China, who would obliterate them——

Mr. PERRY. Would Iran use or could they use North Korean territory to test, to store, to—for instance, in the agreement, there is a discussion or at least a point of a multiport explosive device.

Ms. ROSETT. Multipoint detonation, yes.

Mr. PERRY. Right, for nuclear purposes. Now, I watched the Secretary of Energy today say that would not be allowed, yet in the agreement, it says that the Commission will facilitate their use of that. Is that something that would be—well, I guess they can do it in Iran based on the agreement.

Ms. ROSETT. They can do it if it is watched and surveyed, but it is an excellent question. There is already speculation that Iran may have received test data from North Korea's tests. In testimony to this committee last year, former—an Obama administration official Glyn Davies was asked, would the two cooperate, Iran and North Korea, on nuclear test data? He said they would have every incentive to do so.

Mr. PERRY. What is Russia's relationship with North Korea as it relates to Iran and this situation with their nuclear, the peaceful program?

Ms. ROSETT. Yeah, Russia has become much, much friendlier with North Korea. Russia built the reactor to begin with. Russia delights right now in frustrating the United States. Russia doesn't—North Korea is not going to launch a nuclear attack on Russia, okay. Russia is very happy with what is happening with North Korea right now.

And may I add, there is considerable reason why Iran might use North Korea for a nuclear test site. There is no other country in the world in the 21st century that has conducted nuclear tests. It is conspicuous when you do that. North Korea has done three. They have threatened a fourth since last year. And it would be the best way you could possibly hide a test in plain sight. And it is very easy. You don't need Iranians sitting there on the bleachers. All you need is a thumb drive to——

Mr. PERRY. Forgive me.

Dr. Walsh, so I listened to your testimony, which seemed to countervail everybody else on the panel here.

Mr. WALSH. I am the minority witness.

Mr. PERRY. But based on what we have heard here, you feel completely comfortable, it is absolutely zero. I think that is what your characterization was, zero evidence of collaboration between North Korea and Iran?

Mr. WALSH. Well, on nuclear, that is what the Congressional Research Service says. And as I pointed out, at no point has the DNI, the U.N. Panel of Experts for Iran, the U.N. Panel of Experts for North Korea, or IAEA ever made that claim. I would encourage you all if you have doubts about it, simply call the DNI into a closed session and ask.

Mr. PERRY. Doctor——

Mr. NIKSCH. I wrote for the Congressional Research Service, and my report, which I believe you have, "North Korea Nuclear Weapons Development and Diplomacy," which I wrote and updated from 2007 to 2012, contains a section on nuclear collaboration with Iran and Syria. And if you read that, it goes to the point I made that to find out about this, you are not going to hear it from State Department or even the U.S. intelligence community for the most part.

Mr. PERRY. Why?

Mr. NIKSCH. There is a policy—again, going back to the Bush administration—of what I would call issue avoidance and nondisclosure about the Iranian-North Korean relationship.

Mr. PERRY. Thank you, Mr. Chair, I yield.

Mr. SHERMAN. There is a policy on issue avoidance?

Mr. NIKSCH. Issue avoidance and nondisclosure.

Mr. POE. That is a policy?

Mr. NIKSCH. Yes.

Mr. SHERMAN. Mr. Chairman, I think that is called the mushroom policy.

Mr. NIKSCH. The State Department constantly issues statements that North Korea is not involved in any state support of terrorist groups and therefore should not go back on the official U.S. list of terrorism-supporting organizations. But in 2011, Secretary of Defense, then Secretary of Defense Gates, gave a speech in San Francisco——

Mr. POE. Excuse me, Dr. Niksch. The Chair reclaims the time with just one question. But your report will be made part of this record, without objection.

Mr. NIKSCH. His speech was a lot different than the denials from the State Department.

Mr. POE. All right, I am going to recognize Mr. Yoho from Florida for his 5 minutes.

Mr. YOHO. Thank you, Mr. Chairman.

And I will probably come back to you Dr. Niksch in a minute.

But, first, I want to go to Dr. Walsh. You were saying there is no evidence that North Korea has helped Iran, and there is no conclusive evidence according to the DNI, but yet, Mr. Frantz's article and research says that they were over there, they were working in 2003, and that is the period of time when there is evidence of a nuclear trigger detonation maybe. And the IAEA has got a 14-page annex, pretty conclusive that there was a major explosion, possibly a nuclear trigger device that was backed up by 1,000 pages of documents from Iran. And for you to say that there is no evidence, I think there is plenty of evidence out there.

And then you said we have anywhere, any time, anyplace, and I have heard John Kerry say that same thing. And yet we know that is not true because it is only time anywhere is if Iran says it is okay. And the secret deal that we found out from Tom Cotton and Mr. Pompeo, talked that—they brought this to light, and we know that through the IAEA, there is an agreement. And it is private between them and Iran, and it is with their permission. And you were talking about, we have access to environmental sampling. That is not true. The environmental sampling is done by Iran, and, you know, as Senator Menendez said today, that would be like having Lance Armstrong pull his own blood sample. I mean, let's get real here. This is a bad deal. And for you to say that this is a good deal for America and the rest of the world, I find that disingenuous because this administration has backed us into a corner going to the U.N. and saying that if we pull out, it is all on us. And I think that is bad for us, it is bad for the world.

And with the North Korea deal that was done, Japan and South Korea wanted the deal because it affected them very strongly, and we went along with that deal.

On this deal, none of our Middle Eastern partners were there. Israel wasn't there. None of them want it. And we went ahead with this. It just doesn't make any sense. What are your thoughts on—just on North Korea working with Iran?

Mr. WALSH. Well, on several different things. On the Frantz report, as I say in my written statement, historically—and I am the person here who is, you know, that is what I do in my scholarship is look at the nuclear histories in states that start down the path, stop and reverse course—media reports have proven incredibly unreliable. I will take the DNI every day of the week. Any time or anywhere inspection is in the additional protocol, it has been in the additional protocol; it has been exercised. It is not a secret deal. Yes, it is confidential. That is normal regular operating procedure for the agency.

This is not the first time they have dealt with this situation. When South Africa denuclearized, they went in. It was confidential. When the U.S. shows nuclear stuff to the IAEA we don't give the Russian Duma access to that report. For the agency to do its work, it has to—which is with sovereign states—it has to maintain confidentiality to be the effective. Bad for the——

Mr. YOHO. I am going to interrupt you though. We pay 25 percent of the budget for the IAEA, and if we are paying that much, I want to know the information because we are supposed to vote on a deal. And Secretary Kerry said we are going to get briefed on it. That doesn't cut it for me. I want the information, so we can make our own decision.

I am going to go to Dr. Niksch now.

Do you have any evidence that the missiles you were talking about from North Korea or any other military specifically for nuclear weapons, being conducted between Iran and North Korea, do you have any information on that for sure, that we know there is transfer there or has been in the past?

Mr. NIKSCH. Certainly with regard to the Nodong intermediate-range missile that I have mentioned. The Shabab-3 missiles that Iran produced contain significant components of the North Korean Nodong. And North Korea and Iran from, again, numerous reports, citing European, German, Israeli defense and intelligence officials, that collaboration in trying to improve the Nodong and Shahab-3 missiles has continued.

Mr. YOHO. Okay.

Mr. NIKSCH. Every North Korean missile test since 2006 has seen, reportedly, Iranian delegations in North Korea to observe those tests and undoubtedly get the data from those tests.

Mr. YOHO. All right, thank you. And I heard John Kerry say this multiple times, that you can't bomb knowledge out of the people. And you said that. But you sure dang sure can bomb the will out of them, and I am not advocating more, but if we would have negotiated from a power—or position of strength, we would be in a better situation, and I think we would all be safer 5 years from now.

And this deal will go through, possibly, and when it does, you know, it is going to be hanging on somebody's reputation. You know, they will either be the next Chamberlain in history, or if they are lucky, they will be the next Reagan. See you.

Mr. POE. I want to thank all of our witnesses. Excellent testimony. I wish we could go on for a longer time, and I appreciate your willingness to continue talking about this.

And, Ms. Rosett, I want to especially thank you for your work that you did in the U.N. Oil-for-Food program, the scandal, and revealing that.

This concludes the hearing of the three subcommittees, and the three subcommittees are adjourned. Thank you.

[Whereupon, at 4:35 p.m., the subcommittees were adjourned.]

APPENDIX

MATERIAL SUBMITTED FOR THE RECORD

JOINT SUBCOMMITTEE HEARING NOTICE
COMMITTEE ON FOREIGN AFFAIRS
U.S. HOUSE OF REPRESENTATIVES
WASHINGTON, DC 20515-6128

Subcommittee on Terrorism, Nonproliferation, and Trade
Ted Poe (R-TX), Chairman

Subcommittee on Asia and the Pacific
Matt Salmon (R-AZ), Chairman

Subcommittee on the Middle East and North Africa
Ileana Ros-Lehtinen (R-FL), Chairman

TO: MEMBERS OF THE COMMITTEE ON FOREIGN AFFAIRS

You are respectfully requested to attend an OPEN hearing of the Committee on Foreign Affairs, to be held jointly by the Subcommittee on Terrorism, Nonproliferation, and Trade, the Subcommittee on Asia and the Pacific, and the Subcommittee on the Middle East and North Africa in Room 2172 of the Rayburn House Office Building (and available live on the Committee website at http://www.ForeignAffairs.house.gov):

DATE: Tuesday, July 28, 2015

TIME: 3:00 p.m.

SUBJECT: The Iran-North Korea Strategic Alliance

WITNESSES: Mr. Ilan Berman
                    Vice President
                    American Foreign Policy Council

                    Ms. Claudia Rosett
                    Journalist-in-Residence
                    Foundation for Defense of Democracies

                    Larry Niksch, Ph.D.
                    Senior Associate
                    Center for Strategic and International Studies

                    Jim Walsh, Ph.D.
                    Research Associate
                    Security Studies Program
                    Massachusetts Institute of Technology

By Direction of the Chairman

The Committee on Foreign Affairs seeks to make its facilities accessible to persons with disabilities. If you are in need of special accommodations, please call 202/225-5021 at least four business days in advance of the event, whenever practicable. Questions with regard to special accommodations in general (including availability of Committee materials in alternative formats and assistive listening devices) may be directed to the Committee.

85

COMMITTEE ON FOREIGN AFFAIRS

MINUTES OF SUBCOMMITTEE ON <u>*Terrorism Nonproliferation and Trade; Asia and the Pacific; Middle East and North Africa*</u> HEARING

Day___*Tuesday*___Date___*July 28, 2015*___Room_____*2172*_____

Starting Time ____*3:03 p.m.*____Ending Time ___*4:35 p.m.*___

Recesses |____| (____to____)(____to____)(____to____)(____to____)(____to____)(____to____)

Presiding Member(s)

Chairman Ted Poe

Check all of the following that apply:

Open Session ☑   Electronically Recorded (taped) ☑
Executive (closed) Session ☐   Stenographic Record ☑
Televised ☑

TITLE OF HEARING:

"The Iran-North Korea Strategic Alliance"

SUBCOMMITTEE MEMBERS PRESENT:

Reps. Poe, Salmon, Ros-Lehtinen, Rohrabacher, Duncan, Cook, Weber, Yoho, Chabot, Perry, Keating, Sherman, Deutch, Connolly, Gabbard

NON-SUBCOMMITTEE MEMBERS PRESENT: *(Mark with an * if they are not members of full committee.)*

HEARING WITNESSES: Same as meeting notice attached? Yes ☑ No ☐
(If "no", please list below and include title, agency, department, or organization.)

STATEMENTS FOR THE RECORD: *(List any statements submitted for the record.)*

TIME SCHEDULED TO RECONVENE _____
or
TIME ADJOURNED ___*4:35 p.m.*___

_____
Subcommittee Staff Director